A FREE PEOPLE

OUR STORIES, OUR VOICES, OUR DREAMS

PRODUCED BY THE HMONG YOUTH CULTURAL AWARENESS PROJECT

On the cover:

Though Hmong pa ndau designs may vary from one person to another, they contain the same distinct patterns and symbols. Pictured on the cover is a White Hmong design. Some would interpret the shape as an elephant foot. Others refer to its swirls as snails or "qaaj qwj."

The "snail" spiral is a natural form which recalls the Hmong view of life as a circle.

A Free People:
Our Stories, Our Voices, Our Dreams

Published by the Hmong Youth Cultural Awareness Project through a grant from the Minneapolis Public Schools, Minneapolis, Minnesota. John Mundahl, Dave Moore and Yee Chang, coordinators.

Published by
The Hmong Youth Cultural Awareness Project
5317 York Avenue South
Minneapolis, MN 55410

ISBN 0-9641869-0-X (paper bound)

PRINTED AND BOUND IN THE UNITED STATES OF AMERICA
GRACELAND GRAPHICS, MINNEAPOLIS, MINNESOTA.
First Edition.
0 9 8 7 6 5 4 3 2 1

Dedication

_____

To our parents and grandparents,
our brothers and sisters,
our friends– all those who lost the way
or were turned back,
those who guided us and protected us,
who fought and died
so that we could find refuge and a future
here in this new land.

Acknowledgements

The Hmong Youth Cultural Awareness Project was made possible through a grant from the Minneapolis Public Schools. The project spanned the 1993-1994 school year, during which time this book was written.

We are grateful to the people whose contributions made this book a reality. Westminster Presbyterian Church provided a space for HYCAP meetings. John Mundahl and Dave Moore lent vision and guidance to the project, from writing the grant proposal to proof-reading final galleys of the book. Tim Ready, Curator, Anthropology Department of the Science Museum of Minnesota, provided knowledge and insight into Hmong artifacts as well as numerous pa ndau photos. The St. Paul Pioneer Press, Minneapolis Southwest High School and Tim Montgomery facilitated the book's layout and production.

The following members of HYCAP each contributed stories, art work, or otherwise a great deal of time to this book: Dan Hess, Yee Chang, Tong Thao, Kao Vang, Pang Xiong, Bruce Xiang, Alee Chang, Mai Nhia Xiong, Gkao Vang, Betty Chang, Paul Yang, Koua Her, Va Vang, Moo Vu, Chua Chang, Mai See Xiong, Shu Yang, Yimeem Vu, Doua Chang, and Doua Thao. Others include: Su Thao, Chu Vu, Mai Nhia Yang, Yia Vang, and Choua Vang.

We would especially like to thank our parents and elders whose stories and wisdom are recorded here to be passed on to a new generation of Hmong.

Contents

Foreword

This book was written by the Hmong youth of Minneapolis. The authors, 14-18-year-old students in the Minneapolis Public Schools, met throughout the 1993-1994 school year.

Their book tells the story of the Hmong through the eyes, and in the voices of these courageous young people. These young men and women are now struggling to find meaning in their new American culture, as well as in their traditional Hmong culture, which is quickly fading from their memory.

Many of us teaching and working with Hmong youth in the Minneapolis Public Schools have been touched by their stories of courage and survival. The desire of our Hmong students to learn about their own past led David Moore and me to apply for the grant which made this book possible. The purpose of the grant was to place Hmong youth in touch with their elders, and to record the conversations and collective wisdom that traditionally was passed from one generation to another.

Through the winter, we met weekly at Westminster Church in downtown Minneapolis to produce this book. Between meetings, the group members interviewed elders, researched history, photographed Hmong celebrations, and wrote about their most personal fears and dreams of life in their new country.

I would like to thank Yee Chang, project youth coordinator, for his leadership, the adult advisors for giving freely of their time, Westminster Church for giving us a room in which to meet, the Minneapolis Public Schools for funding the grant, the Science Museum of Minnesota for providing us with photographs of artifacts, the St. Paul Pioneer Press for letting us use their computer system to lay-out the book, and of course, the wonderful young Hmong men and women for writing and illustrating this book. Congratulations!

John Mundahl
Minneapolis Public Schools
Author of "Tales of Courage, Tales of Dreams"
May 1, 1994
Minneapolis, Minnesota

The Hmong are a mountain people who have traditionally practiced slash-and-burn agriculture combined with crossbow and home-made rifles. Always a minority in every country where they have lived, they value their independence and self-sufficiency. The word "Hmong" means "free people."

The Hmong originally lived in China, migrating the mid-1800s to northern Laos. There, they farmed peacefully in the high mountains for over one hundred years. During the Vietnam War, thousands of Hmong soldiers fought for the United States against North Vietnam. When the war ended, more than 100,000 Hmong men, women and children were killed by Pathet Lao and North Vietnamese for aiding the U.S. The Hmong fled their mountain villages in Laos for refuge in Thailand. More than half the fleeing refugees died trying to escape. Those who reached Thailand arrived in a state of physical collapse and emotional shock. They had left nearly everything behind for a life in crowded and unsanitary camps along the Thai border, waiting for an opportunity to settle in third countries like the U.S. Many Hmong people spent over ten years in these camps, living off little more than rumors and hope. The U.S. has granted many asylum because of their crucial role in the Vietnam War, but the Hmong have had great difficulty adjusting to a culture so different from their own.

Minnesota now has the second largest Hmong population in America with almost 20,000 refugees. Eighty percent live in the twin cities of Minneapolis and St. Paul and surrounding communities. The Minneapolis Public Schools Limited English Proficiency Program is two-thirds Hmong. These young people are facing tremendous challenges as they struggled in a state of transition from traditional Hmong ways to an adopted American culture. In the process, many have become alienated from both cultures.

Dr. Yang Dao, a nationally-known Hmong leader residing in the Twin Cities area, writes: "Hmong teenagers, uprooted from their own culture and thrown into the middle of an industrial society for which they are not prepared, find themselves torn between two different worlds: the world of the Hmong traditional society, about which they know almost nothing; and the new world of American society which is still incomprehensible to them.

"Hmong children who are born or grow up in the United States," he continues, "must be better prepared to confront culture shock. This preparation must include a better knowledge of their (own) culture and traditions. Appreciation of their native culture's moral and human values will be a springboard for them to perceive a new culture with a better sense of judgment."

Educators and social scientists know that culture protects youth. Kathy Wealdon states that we must recognize that culture itself is "an undersold solution to youth-related problems." She goes on, "all youth must be taught their cultural heritage." Hugh Vasquez writes that "learning one's culture is the act of developing the social, moral (and) intellectual faculties that will provide individuals with tools for healthy functioning." It was for this reason that John Mundahl and myself, teachers in the Minneapolis public schools, decided to set up a program that would give Hmong youth the opportunity to examine their cultural roots by putting them back in touch with parents and elders. We have been at it now for almost an entire school year. We have learned about Hmong culture, and we have learned about each other. It has been a tremendously rewarding journey for all of us.

Dave Moore
Author of "Dark Sky, Dark Land," Scoutmaster and former teacher
Minneapolis, April 11, 1994

Prologue

When I first started meeting Hmong kids in 1981, I was taken by the stories they told of their struggle to survive. They would tell, hesitantly, usually with a smile, about the hardship of life on the run, about the fears of leaving home and family behind, and about the anticipated dangers of life in America. In all ways I was impressed by their courage, and by their sense of community.

I heard first-hand accounts from children who'd seen family members shot dead in front of them as they scrambled for cover. I heard about a family living underground in a hole for a year, afraid to come out, afraid of being killed. I heard about parents and children forever separated, torn apart in the treacherous currents of the Mekong River.

We were sitting around a Boy Scout campfire when I first heard about the monsters that the Hmong people feared would eat them when they got to America.

"Monsters?!, " I said.

"Yes." The Scouts said, "Monsters that eat Hmong people."

I wanted to know how they could actually believe that monsters lived here. They said that they'd heard stories from the old people in the

■ By Dan Hess, Assistant Scoutmaster of Boy Scout Troop 100 and a volunteer with the Hmong Youth Cultural Awareness Project. (Illustration from a drawing by Paul Yang)

11

camps in Thailand.

"Monsters, indeed," I thought. How could rational adults believe in man-eating monsters and why would they frighten their children with this nonsense?

We talked about the monsters' preferred diet of Hmong flesh. I thought this was funny, but when I laughed, I laughed alone.

That was more than ten years ago and I was certain that I'd never seen a monster in America, and I assured my young friends not to worry.

I wish I still had that confidence. Since then, I've heard little talk about the monsters that live in America, but recently I've found myself thinking about them, a lot.

A couple of months ago as I was driving a van-load of Hmong Scouts home, we passed the corner where a Hmong youth, a former Boy Scout, was beaten with baseball bats almost to death by rival gang members. At that time I was told he was in the hospital and was not expected to live.

We talked about gang violence, about other difficulties that Hmong kids face, and about what it's like to be a Hmong in America, to feel caught between two cultures.

"Do you guys ever hear about the monsters that live in America?" I asked.

"Monsters?" they said, in disbelief.

"Yes. The first Scouts in Troop 100 used to tell me about the monsters that live in America and eat Hmong people."

A wave of laughter passed through the van, but there was no laughter in me. I slipped into silence and was lost in thought, finding my way out only to say "good night" to each of my Scouts as they arrived at their homes, one-by-one.

I thought about the stories of their struggle for survival, about life on the run from violence, about their fears of leaving the safety of their homes, about the dangers they face from life in America.

From these young Scouts I've heard stories about kids shot dead in front of their friends; about families staying indoors, afraid of being killed; about parents and children forever separated, torn apart by the treacherous currents of life in America, a life deluded by the seductive ethic of individual consumerism.

I've seen the monsters that eat Hmong people in America, and I don't feel much like laughing.

I've also seen in these Hmong people, in my young friends, the strength of collective courage and mutual support.

They will need it, once again, in their latest struggle to survive. ▼

A Brief History

A thousand years ago, Hmong ancestors were said to have lived in Mongolia. This was their original homeland. In ancient times, before they began migrating south into China, the Hmong religion was an ancestor worship similar to that of the Mongolians. When sick, we sought help from a shaman to guide our spirit back to health. Later, when we migrated to China, we brought this religion with us. The Hmong and the Mongolian people share some similarities since we were a subgroup within the Mongolian family. The Hmong in Mongolia raised horses, buffaloes and bulls. The latter two were used for fighting. The Hmong were expert horsemen and they held spectacular races, much like the Mongolian people.

In 2500 B.C., the Chinese conquered the Mongol homeland. The Hmong could no longer live there and fled south. Our ancestors settled on the Yellow River in what is now the northeast region of China. According to some Chinese records, we were the first people to live there. We lived in China for a thousand years. We were the first people to use bronze and to developed an irrigation system. We also raised fish. At that time, the Hmong had a king. He had good laws to protect our people and our country.

During that time, the Han Chinese were a nomadic people who came from the west to settle on the Yellow River near our people. They were friendly for a long time, but Chinese culture is different from Hmong culture – they use chopsticks; we use spoons. One day, a Han Chinese asked the Hmong to let their sons and daughters marry into the Chinese culture. The Hmong did not agree to do so. Our ancestors were afraid they would lose their culture and language because there were many more Chinese than Hmongs.

When the area was conquered by the Chin dynasty around 214 B.C., the Hmong abandoned their homes on the Yellow River and moved into south-central China. They settled along the Yangtze River and started a new life. Before our people could rebuild, the Chinese attacked again from the north. They killed thousands of Hmong. They said they would kill all the Hmong men and all the baby boys, but would leave the women. Our ancestors couldn't risk more lives, so they rebelled against the Chinese.

In the final battle, the Hmong king was killed and our kingdom was lost. Many Hmong had no choice but to flee further south into

Kang Neng Xiang

■ *This short history is related by Kang Neng Xiang, the father of HYCAP member Bruce Xiang. He traces the Hmong from their roots in China to resettlement in the highlands of Laos, Thailand, Vietnam and Burma.*

what is now Burma, Thailand, Laos, and Vietnam. But not all of the Hmong left; some remained in China. There are approximately eight million still there today. There are many ethnic groups in southern China whose origins are Hmong, or closely related. T he Chinese refer to them as Miao.

The Hmong that fled south settled in the highlands of Laos, Vietnam, Thailand, and Burma because there was no other empty land available. Once again, we had to start building a new life. We farmed and raised animals for food. We worked hard every day, and there was no government to help us. Some villages had no time to celebrate the New Year.

In the 1940s, the Hmong in Laos were recruited to work for the American CIA. The CIA wanted the Hmong to help fight the North Vietnamese, and in exchange the Americans promised General Vang Pao that they would help protect and rebuild the Hmong homeland. They further promised that if the Americans lost the war, they would get the Hmong out of Laos. They did lose the war in 1975, and the Hmong became refugees once again. About two million Hmong lived in Southeast Asia before the Vietnam War. Many died.

Today, most of the Hmong living in the United States are refugees from Laos. ▼

▼▼▼

There are more than six million Hmong in the world. Their voices ring out in variations of the same tongue from the southern provinces of China, the mountains of Laos, Vietnam, and Thailand, from France, Australia, Canada, and the United States.

A peaceful and free people, we became the first enemy of the Chinese. We were different in many ways from the other Asian groups. Odd looking, enemies, too, for some Hmong were blond and blue eyed. Such Hmong are still to be found, though they are few in number. French anthropologist and priest, Father Savina believed the Hmong were remnants of a Caucasian group from Southern Russia or the Iranian Plateau. Where our origins begin, we have no records of, just stories and legends passed down from one generation to another.

My ancestors were forced out of China nearly two hundred years ago because they would not bow down to Chinese ways. They would not and could not stop being Hmong. They wanted to be let alone, to be free, as the word "Hmong" confirms.

Anthropologists called us nomads, mountain dwellers, primitive people. We had no choice but to keep moving, to isolate and hide ourselves in places inaccessible to suppressive forces. In Southeast Asia, we found a new home in the high altitudes of Laos and Vietnam, removed and freed from trouble.

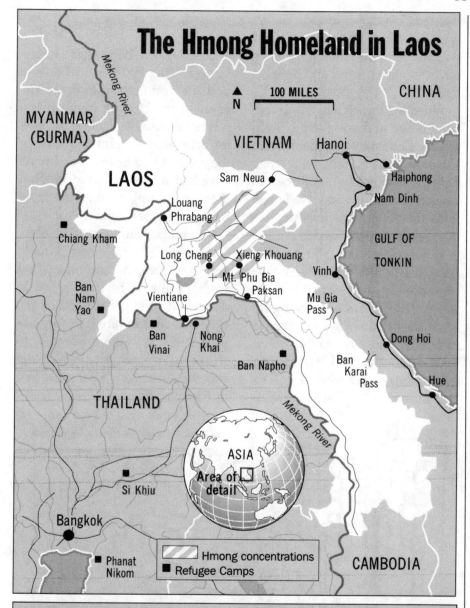

The Hmong Homeland in Laos

100 MILES

CHINA

MYANMAR (BURMA)

VIETNAM

Hanoi

LAOS

Sam Neua

Haiphong

Nam Dinh

Louang Phrabang

Chiang Kham

Long Cheng

Xieng Khouang

GULF OF TONKIN

Vinh

Ban Nam Yao

+ Mt. Phu Bia

Paksan

Vientiane

Mu Gia Pass

Ban Vinai

Nong Khai

Ban Napho

Dong Hoi

Ban Karai Pass

Hue

THAILAND

Mekong River

ASIA

Area of detail

Si Khiu

Bangkok

Phanat Nikom

Hmong concentrations
Refugee Camps

CAMBODIA

Map locates the Hmong homeland in Laos centered in the mountains of Xieng Khouang Province.

Hmong Chronology

■ **About 2500 B.C.:** Hmong begin to migrate into China from Mongolia.

■ **B.C. 214.:** The Hmong of south central China are conquered by the Ch'in dynasty.

■ **1600s:** French catholic priests are first Europeans to encounter Hmong.

■ **1700s:** At least four major Hmong rebellions are crushed by China's Manchu dynasty.

■ **1800s:** Hmong in greater numbers and French move into Laos.

■ **1954:** Fall of Dienbienphu ends French presence in Indo-China.

■ **1965:** U.S. combat troops in Vietnam utilize Hmong bases, troops in Laos.

■ **1975:** Fall of Vietnam to Communist forces; Hmong exodus from Laos.

SOURCE: Dark Sky Dark Land by David L. Moore.

15

But that was soon to change. We were contacted by the French and was made to bow down to them, pay them taxes, work and fight for them.

When the French left, the Americans came and sought our help against Communist expansion from Vietnam. The Hmong were good fighters, having fought for freedom for thousands of years. We fought with the Americans for our freedom and American freedom.

When elders talk about life in Laos, it wasn't life they were talking about, it was war and death. After many years of fighting for what they had always believed in as freedom, they found themselves back where they had started three generations earlier when they were first pushed out of China: poor, re-pressed, and still longing for freedom.

On May 9th 1975, after Hmong General Vang Pao fled to Thailand and the communist overran the country, the Hmong found themselves defenseless against the enemy who were determined to wipe them out. Once again, the Hmong have had to flee or face death, but there was no place to go, no more mountains to retreat to.

It is ironic that we call ourselves "free people" while our parents and grandparents remind us that we have always been subjected to domination and persecution by the Chinese. And in recent history, we were subjects to the lowland Laotians, the invading communists, and the Americans who promised us freedom. ▼

■ *A pattern of center diamonds drawn by Tong Thao.*

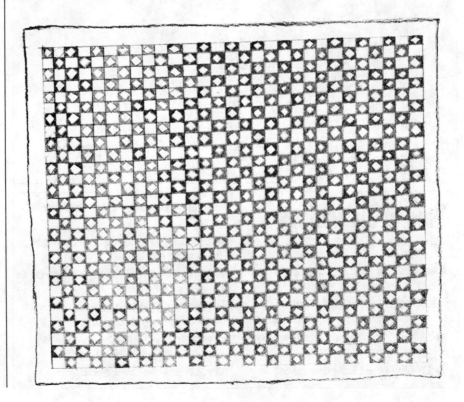

PART ONE

HMONG CULTURE

- ▶ CLAN NAMES
- ▶ FOLK TALES
- ▶ RELIGION
- ▶ HMONG MEDICINE
- ▶ HOUSE DESIGN
- ▶ LUS HMOOB/HMONG LANGUAGE
- ▶ MUSIC
- ▶ LOVE AND MARRIAGE
- ▶ PA NDAU/COSTUMES
- ▶ THE NEW YEAR CELEBRATION

The sun and the moon

L ou Tou was the first man. See Chee was his wife. The first man and woman came out of a mountain. They opened a door and came out. They looked around. They looked up and saw nothing. There was no sun or moon. Everything was dark. The sky was low and Lou Tou could touch it with his hand. Every night was dark. And every day was dark, too.

After a period of time, See Chee got pregnant. She had a son. Then she had two more sons. One of the sons was Teng Chu. He said, "The world is too small. We should make it bigger because people need a bigger place to live."

So then, Teng Chu and his father tapped their feet three times and Teng Chu pushed up the sky. He stretched out the earth. He made a gold lamp for the day and said it was the sun. He made a silver lamp for the night and said it was the moon. Then he hung the sun and the moon up very high.

The sun and moon are in the sky now. And there is light in our sky. ▼

■ *A popular Hmong story about the beginning of the world, as related by Alee Chang.*

17

Clan Names

Mai Nhia Xiong

■ *Mai Nhia is an eighth grade student at Folwell Jr. High School in Minneapolis. Photo at right, taken in the 1960s, includes three generations of the Xiong clan. Mai Nhia's father, Vang Xue Xiong, age 15, is seated on the left. (Xiong family photo)*

"Our last name is very important because it means family."

There are many stories about how the Hmong first got their clan names. This is one story I heard.

A long time ago, there was only one Hmong man and his wife. They had many children. But the children were all brothers and sisters. The man and his wife wanted the Hmong to become a great nation. There was only one thing to do, even though they knew that it was wrong for their children. It was the only way to make the family bigger. They decided to give each of the children a different name. They were given a first name and a clan name. In this way, the children could marry one another.

Since then, our clan names have been passed down from generation to generation. To this day, the Hmong still use the same clan names.

It is important to keep our last name. People who have the same last name are considered brothers and sisters. They can't marry each other. If they do, the family would lose face. They have to look for someone who has a different last name.

When a child is born, he or she takes the father's last name. And it can't be changed. For that reason, Hmong women keep their last names when they get married. ▼

Hmong clan names

Hmong clan names, or last names, are an important part of Hmong life. They are passed down from generation to generation. Today, there are approximately 18 different clan names:

English spelling	Hmong spelling
1. Chang (Cha)	Tsaab
2. Cheng	Tsheej
3. Chue	Tswb
4. Fang	Faaj
5. Hang	Haam
6. Her	Hawj
7. Khang	Khaab
8. Kong	Koo
9. Kue	Kwm
10. Lee (Ly)	Lis
11. Lor (Lo)	Lauj
12. Moua	Muas
13. Pha	Phab
14. Thao	Thoj
15. Vang	Vaaj
16. Vue (Vu)	Vwj
17. Xiong	Xyooj
18. Yang	Yaaj

Folk Tales

A Selfish Family of Six

Once there was a family of six. But they were very selfish. Whenever they had ceremonies and parties, they never invited their relatives to come and celebrate with them. One day they decided to leave the village and move far away. Their new home was three mountains away from the village of their relatives. When they arrived in the middle of the jungle, they stopped and built themselves a new home.

The oldest son and the father set out into the forest to hunt for food. While they were out hunting, they

■ *Doua Thao is 14 years old and a member of Boy Scout Troop 100. He likes to tell Hmong stories and folk tales (dab neeg) to fellow Scouts around campfires. He knows over one hundred Hmong folk tales. He learned these stories from elders who gathered at funerals, ceremonies, and parties. (Photo by Dan Hess)*

THE TIGER KILLED THE MAN AND ATE HIM

HER HEARD THE CRUNCH

■ *In the folk tales that Doua tells, there are many references to ghosts. Hmong people believe that there many kinds of spirits. In the spirit world, Doua says, a ghost usually takes the form of a tiger. Tigers are usually the king's subordinates. The ghosts are the tigers' wives and slaves. He may order them to make someone sick and to lead the person's spirit to him. And if the ghosts disobey, the tiger eats them. (Pa ndau photo courtesy of the Science Museum of Minnesota)*

encountered a ghost. They were frightened and ran back home, and the ghost chased them all the way home. After a while, the father got very sick and was going to die. When the father knew that he was going to die, he said to his wife, "My wife, when I die I want you to bury me inside of the living room wall."

After the father died, and the funeral was over, the oldest son died too. Night came, and everyone was afraid. The mother tried to wake up the oldest daughter, but she was in a deep sleep and couldn't be awakened. There were two other kids, the youngest one was two years old. The mother looked around and saw a big black tiger at the front door. She turned back towards the living room where the bodies of her husband and son were lying and saw that they were still there. As she looked closer, she saw the rotten juice dripping from the two corpses. It made a haunting sound as it hit the dry-earth floor.

The mother stood there very still and then watched as her dead hus-

band picked up the chicken beside his head (cooked chickens were used in a ceremony to feed the dead) and ate it. When he finished, he tossed the bones aside and picked up the one by his feet and ate that, too. By this time, the mother was numb with fear. She knew that her dead husband would also eat the whole family because he had become a tiger ghost.

She had a plan. She got in front of her loom and started to weave. That made some noise so the husband thought that she was up and awake. But when she stopped weaving, the husband reached out his hands. So she again began weaving and making noise on the loom, and the dead father became still again.

Without a sound, the mother took the youngest child and put him on her back. She climbed to the attic of the house and put him there. The older child could not be awakened so the mother let her sleep where she was. The mother tied a long yarn to the loom so that when she and her third child escaped out of the house. She could pull on the yarn, and the loom would sound as if she was there working. Then she and her child ran and ran as fast as they could back to their former village. But after she climbed over only one mountain, the yarn ran out and the loom stopped.

The father woke up with his mouth full of blood. He said, "My wife, where is everybody?" He got up and looked around and saw his

20

dead son lying next to him. His daughter was still deep in her sleep, so he walked over and starting eating her. When he got to her bones, he made loud, crunching sounds. The two-year-old in the attic heard the sounds and said, "Father, what are you eating?" The father answered, "I'm eating a midnight snack." The father then tried to get into the attic, but he got stuck on the ladder because he was still tied to two long poles that were used to hold his body for the funeral. He looked around and saw the long piece of yarn attached to the loom leading out the door. He realized what the mother had done, and chased after her.

The mother was still running, and when she turned back to look, she saw the two red eyes of her dead husband on top of the mountain behind her. When she got to the top of the next mountain, he had reached the bottom of the valley behind her. So she ran and ran until she finally arrived at the edge of her family's village. The village dogs barked loud, and woke up the whole village. They saw a black fig-

There are many versions of this story about the tiger eating a family. At left is the youngest girl hiding in the attic.

(Pa ndau photos courtesy of the Science Museum of Minnesota)

ure carrying a baby, running toward them. A few moments later, they saw a bigger figure with two red eyes chasing after the first. The mother shouted for help. Her brothers and relatives heard her, got their guns and waited.

When the mother reached her family, she cried so hard that she couldn't tell them anything. They laid her down to rest.

While the village was busy with the mother and child, the father had transformed himself into a human and walked up to the door of her family's house. He knocked on the door, and they opened it. They knew that he was already dead, but they said, "Hi. We see that you are tired from running here, so let's set the table and have dinner." They gave him cooked meat, but he would not eat it. He took the plate with raw meat and ate it instead.

The family asked him, "Why do you eat only raw meat?"

He answered, "Because we live in the forest, sometimes we can't start a fire. So we eat raw meat

21

> **"**These stories are important to me because they give a lot of information about our Hmong history. It is important to tell them and pass them on to the next generation. They teach us many lessons. They teach people to do good, and the consequences of wrong, or bad deeds. Stories tell us about ourselves and where we come from. **"**
> *– Doua Thao*

most of the time."

The mother's younger sister brought the dead father a cup of water. But when she walked over to him, she accidentally stepped on something. He gave a big roar – a sound unlike any human would make. She had stepped on his tail. The family was frightened, but said nothing.

The night passed on into morning. Because a ghost cannot maintain the human form when it is exposed to sunlight, the father had to leave before dawn. He said, "My father-in-law, morning is coming and I have to be going home. In a while, can you tell my wife and child to come home? I have work for them to do."

One day later, the mother finally woke up and told everyone what had happened back home. The relatives got spears and brought their dogs to the her house. When they arrived, they found the two-year-old still alive in the attic. But the daughter on the bed had been eaten. They saw that the dead son's body was missing, but the father's body was still lying on its scaffold. One of the relatives then took a wooden wedge and drove it through the heart. The father was finally dead. ▼

The moral of this story is that if you're selfish and unkind, and you move far away from the people who care about you, then if something happens to you, no one will know about it. And when they do, it might be too late.

Hmong/English Narration

Nkauj Muam Nraug Nus

Thaum ub muaj ob tug nus muag. Tus muam hu ua Xyooj Mim. Tus nus hu ua Xyooj Pov. Niam noj qe qauj ces niam tuag lawm nrauj es txiv noj qe tov ces txiv tuaj lawm ntxov. Tseg tau ob tus nus muag nyob xwb. Nkawv nyob nkawv niaj hnub mus ua mab ua suav zog los noj xwb. Cas nkawv nyob nyob cia li tuaj ib nthwd cua. Ces cia li tsis pom tus muam lawm. Tus nus thiaj li nrhiav tus muam rau qhov twg los tsis pom. Nws nrhiav qab ntuj dhau hauv ntuj los tsis pom.

Nws ho nrhiav mus txoj puag pem hauv ntuj ces thiaj li mus pom ib tug pog laus. Tus pog laus hais tias, "Me tub, koj yuav tuaj mus ua dab tsi? Ua cas koj yuav quaj ua luaj?"

Xyooj Pov teb tias, "Niam tais, twb yog niam thiab txiv ob tug tso wb tseg lawm. Wb nyob nyob ces tuaj ib nthwv cua ces tsis pom kuv tus muam lawm xwb. Kuv nrhiav qab ntug hauv ntuj tau peb xyoo no nrhiav tsis pom nws li. Kuv tuaj no ces kuv tuaj nrhiav kuv tus muam xwb tiag."

"Me tub, txhob quaj. Kuv mam li qhia koj mus nrhiav kom tau os mog. Koj taug txoj kev no mus kom txog puag tom lub zos hmoob uas muaj ib yim poj ntsuam. Nws nyob nram qab zos, ces koj mus nkag rau hauv nws tsev. Koj nug nus ces lawv mam li qhia koj mog.

Xyooj Pov thiaj li taug kev mus li tus pog laus hais. Nws mus txog

Brother and Sister

A long time ago, there was a brother and a sister. The sister was named Xiong Mee. The brother was Xiong Pao. Their mother ate rotten eggs and died. Their father ate mixed eggs and he died long ago too. Only the brother and sister were left. They labored every day for survival. One day, a gush of wind whizzed by, and the sister disappeared. The brother looked everywhere, from the bottom of the sky to the top, but his sister was nowhere to be found.

Then he went to the far end of the sky and saw an old lady. She said, "Little boy, what are you doing here? Why are you crying so hard?"

Xiong Pao answered, "Old lady, I am crying because my parents have left us. Then one day a gush of wind whizzed by, and my sister disappeared. I have been looking everywhere under the heavens for three years now, but I still can't find my sister. The reason I came here is to look for my sister.

"Little boy, don't cry. I will tell you how to find your sister – alright? Just follow this road until you get to a Hmong village where a widow lives. Her house is at the lower edge of the village. Go into her house. Then ask her what you came for and she will tell you what to do.

Xiong Pao went on his way as the old lady had told him. He came to

23

puag tom hmoob zos ces thiaj li mus nkag rau hauv ib yim poj ntsuam tsev.

Tus poj tsuam nug tias, "Me tub, koj tuaj dab tsi?"

"Ab, niam tais, twb yog kuv tuaj nrhiav kuv tus muam. Niam thiab txiv yug tau wb ob tug me nus muag xwb. Wb nyob nyob ces tuaj ib nthwv cua ces cia li tsis pom kuv tus muam lawm. Kuv nrhiav qab ntug dhau hauv ntuj tsis pom li.

Poj ntsuam teb tias, "Me tub, txhob quaj. Kuv qhia koj. Koj nyob ntawm no, ib tug nyab niaj hnub tuaj nqa vab tshaus mus tshaus mov noj. Es hle koj cev ris tsho rau kuv. Es kuv li mam muab ib cev rau koj hnav. Ib pliag no nws tuaj kuv sim muab rau nws seb nws puas paub."

Ces Xyooj Pov hle zoj nus cev ris tsho. Poj ntsuam thiaj muab tau ib cev rau nws hnav. Ib me ntsis hnub qaij hlo, Xyooj Mim khiav tuaj hais tias, "Niam tais kuv tuaj qiv koj lub vab tshaus mus tshaus mov no."

"Tau kawg los mas me nyab. Kuv niag laus laus, qhov muag tsis pom kev lawm. Koj tuaj txog lawm ces thov koj pab ntxiv kuv cev khuab ncaws dab dab tuag no rau kuv tau hnav mus ua teb os."

Xyooj Mim teb tias, "Aws, nyob qhov twg muab los rau kuv ntxiv." Xyooj Mim thiaj khaws los muab ntxiv. Nws muab saib sab twg los yog nws cov qab koob uas thaum nws xaws tseg rau nws tus nus hnav xwb. Ces nws ib kev ntxiv ib kev quaj.

Tus niam poj ntsuam thiaj hais tias, "Me nyab, cas zoo li koj quaj

a Hmong village and entered a widow's house at the lower edge of the village.

The widow asked him, "Little boy, what are you doing here?"

"Lady, I came here looking for my sister. My parents had only the two of us as brother and sister. Then one day, a gush of wind whizzed by and my sister disappeared. I looked everywhere under the heavens but she was nowhere to be found.

The widow answered, "Little boy, don't cry. I will tell you how to find her. You stay here. Every day a girl comes to get her rice sifter for preparing dinner. Take off your clothes and leave them to me. I will give you other clothes to wear. In a little while she will come, and I will give your clothes to her to see if she knows.

Xiong Pao took off his clothes and the widow gave him other clothes to wear. Then, just when the sun started to descend, Xiong Mee came running to ask, "Lady, I have come to borrow your rice sifter to prepare dinner."

"Sure, my little daughter-in-law. I am very old and I cannot see anymore. Since you are here, please help me stich up my rags so I can wear them to work in the fields."

Xiong Mee answered, "Sure, where are they? I can stich them up for you." She picked the clothes and saw her own needle work was on the rags. She had sewn the clothes for her brother long ago. She cried and cried as she patched up the rags.

■ *The Hmong believe there is a magical world beneath water.*

25

quaj es yog ua cas?"

"Niam tais, cev ris tsho kuv ntxiv no zoo li ce kuv xaws tseg rau kuv tus nus nyob puag nram Xov Tshoj."

"Ces koj paub lov?"

"Kuv saib mas yog tiag tabsis ntshe tsis yog xwb. Puas yog tiag?," Xyooj Mim nug.

"Yog kawg. Nws tuaj txog qhov no es kuv hais tias muab cev ris tsho rau koj seb koj puas paub."

Ces tus poj tsuam thiaj li mus qhib hlo lub yias uas kwb Xyooj Pov. Xyooj Pov tawm plaws lo.

"Xyooj Mim, ua cas koj los ua neej rau rooj teb no es koj tsis qhia kuv li? Niam thiab txiv yug tau wb ob leeg xwb. Vim li cas koj thiaj khiav lawm? Kuv nrhiav koj tau peb xyoo no. Kuv twb quaj quaj qab ntug dhau hauv ntuj, noj tsis taus ib lub mov haus tsis taus ib ncos dej li. Cas koj siab phem tas npaum? Tsis yog kuv tsis kheev koj yuav txiv, kuv yeej kheev. Koj yog ib leeg khaub ntxais. Kuv yeej cia koj mus yuav txiv xwb."

Ob tus me nus muag xav zoj ces cia li sib qhawg quaj. Tag ntawd ces Xyooj Mim hais Xyooj Pov tias, "koj tuaj txog lawm ces mus pem kuv tsev."

Nws coj Xyooj Pov mus txog nws tsev thiab ua zaub ua mov rau nkawv noj tag.

"Xyooj Pov, koj yawm yij tsiv tsiv tsaim li es kuv muab peb lub yias no khwb koj tseg. Ib me ntsis nws los txog kuv mam li qhia nws txog koj. Yog nws tsis cem no ces kuv mam li tso koj taum los. Yog nws cem koj no ces koj rov qab mus.

The widow asked her, "Daughter-in-law, it looks like you are crying. What is wrong?"

"Lady, the clothes here look like the ones I made for my brother at home in Lower China (Laos)."

"Then you know?"

"From what I can tell, I know. But maybe it's not. Is it true?" Xiong Mee demanded.

"Yes it is. He came here and I told him to look at his clothes to see if you know."

The widow opened up the cooking pan where Xiong had hidden himself, and he jumped out.

"Xiong Mee, why didn't you tell me that you had come to live here? Mother and father had only the two of us. Why did you go away? I have looked for you for three years now. I have been crying everywhere in search of you. I haven't been able to eat a single grain of rice or drink a single drop of water. Why do you have such a bad heart. It's not that I don't want you to get married. I do. You are a girl, and I will let you get married. "

When they came to the realization of how much they had missed each other, the brother and sister hugged and cried. After that, Xiong Mee said to Xiong Pao, "Now that you are here, come to my house."

She took Xiong Pao to her house and fixed a meal for them.

"Xiong Pao, your brother-in-law is very naggy, so I will have to hide you under these three cooking pans. When he comes back, I will tell him about you. If he doesn't scold you then I will let you out. If

Tag kis nws mus ua teb no ces kuv mam tso koj mus tsev mog."

Xyooj Mim muab tau peb lub yias los khwb Xyooj Pov tseg. Ib me ntsis, nws tus txiv ya los txog ntua tsev, txo plhuav nra. Tus txiv nug, "Xyooj Mim, hnub no koj nyob hauv tsev cas yuav tsw hmo nplej hmo nplaum tas npaum li. Yog leej twg tuaj nev?"

"Koj txiv, koj mus ces koj mus noj ntawm koj ncauj tsw ntawm koj ntswg. Kuv nyob hauv tsev nrog ob peb tug menyuam ces kuv twb tsis khoom li."

Zaum zoj ib pliag ces niag txiv rov nug dua. Xyooj Mim saib zoj tsis tau, ntshai tsam niag txiv cem. Nws thiaj li hais tias, "Dag mas dag li, tabsis yog dab laug tuaj es kuv ntshai tsam koj cem dab laug es kuv thiaj tsis qhia koj."

"Cas koj siab phem ua luaj? Koj tseem dag kuv thiab?" tus txiv cem. Nws mus qhib hlo peb lub yias ces dab laug tawm plaws los.

Ces Xyooj Pov nrog yawm yij nyob tau peb hnub. Hnub peb, yawm yij ua tau ib pluag mov rau nws noj. Tas ntawd, nws mus thov Vaj Pej Huam tuaj coj dab laug mus noj mov. Lawv haus dej haus cawv tau peb hnub peb hmo ces Xyooj Pov thiab Vaj Pej Huam nkawd thiaj li qaug qaug cawv.

Ces Vaj Pej Huam hais Xyooj Pov tias,"Yog koj hu tau neeg tawm hauv lub pas dej no tuaj ces kuv mam li nyoo koj. Yog kuv hu tau neeg tawm hauv lub pas dej no ces koj nyoo kuv."

he does, then you will have to go home. He will go to the fields tomorrow, so I will let you go home then."

So, she covered him with three pans. In a short while, her busband came flying into the house and took the load off his back. The husband asked, "Xiong Mee, why do I smell such sweet rice aroma at home today? Who is here?"

"Husband, it's probably just the food smell from your lunch today. I have been home with the children and have had no time for anything else."

The husand sat down a while and later asked again about the aroma of sweet rice. Xiong Mee was afraid that she would be scolded, and answered, "I was only kidding. Your brother-in-law came, but I was afraid you would scold him, so I didn't tell you."

"Why are you so mean? And why did you lie to me?" the husband scolded. He then lifted the pans and the brother jumped out.

Xiong Pao stayed with his brother-in-law for a few days. On the third day, the brother-in-law fixed him a meal. Then he went to ask Vaj Pej Huam to invite his guest for another meal.

They drank for three days and three nights, until Xiong Pao and Vaj Pej Huam were both very drunk.

Then Vaj Pej Huam said to Xiong Pao, "If you can summon people from the bottom of this lake, then I will let you win. And if I can do it, then you lose."

Xyooj Pov teb, "Ua li los us li!"

Vaj Pej Huam hu ua ntej, "Zaj Txwg Zaj Laug, koj sim tawm tuaj saum no kuv muaj lus hais koj." Nws hais peb zaug cas pas dej ntsiag to.

Ces, Xyooj Pov thiaj hu tias, "Zaj Txoo Yig Laus, tuaj cuaj ceg kub yim ceg kos, Tus paub dab paub qhuas, paub ib puas yam tsav, tawm tuaj!" Nws hu peb zaug diam. Hu tas, cas tawm ib lub npuas dej.

Zaum ob, cas lub pas dej ntas ntuav tim ub tim no. Nws hu zaum peb, cas zaj lub tob hau tawm plaws tuaj.

Zaj Laus thiaj li muab Vaj Pej Huam nplawm tuag lawm.

Zaj Laug hais rau Xyooj Pov tias, "Leej kw, cas koj yuav muaj ib tsab xo nyav ncawv tuaj rau kuv los tsev?"

Tus yawm yij hais rau dab laug tias, "Tsis txhob ntshai, ntawm no yog kuv txiv ntag."

Ces Zaj Laus coj Xyooj Pov mus Zaj Laus lub teb chaws hauv qab pas dej uas ci ntsag iab. Zaj Laus nug tias saib Xyooj Pov xav yuav dab tsi. Ces Xyooj Pov tus yawm yij ntxhi hais kom nws yuav tus khaub rhuab xwb. Xyooj Pov tsis paub ces Xyooj Pov teb li nws hais ntawd. Zaj Laus thiaj muab tau niag khaub rhuab rau Xyooj Pov nqa los saum nruab nqhuab no. Los txog saum no cas niag khaub rhuab plhis kiag ua tau Zaj Laus tus ntxhais. Nkawv thiaj li sib yuav ua niam txiv nyob nrog tus muam thiab yawm yij lawm. ▼

Xiong Pao answered, "That will be a deal."

Vaj Pej Huam called out first, "Old dragon, come up to the surface. I have something to say to you." He called out three times, and the lake became silent.

It was Xiong Pao's turn. He called out, "Old dragon with many horns and teeth, he who is wise in tradition and knows it all, come up!" He shouted three times. The first time he called, one air bubble rose to the surface.

The second time, ripples were forming in the lake and splashing back and forth. The third time he called, the dragon's head popped up.

The old dragon came up and whipped Vaj Pej Huam dead.

Then he said to Xiong Pao, "Brother, why do you have such strong message?"

The brother-in-law told Xiong Pao, "Don't be afraid, this guy is my father."

The old dragon took Xiong Pao down to his beautiful and shiny palace under the water. He asked Xiong Pao what he wanted from his palace. Xiong Pao's brother-in-law whispered for him to take only the broom. So, Xiong Pao told the old dragon that all he wanted was the broom. The old dragon gave him the broom and he came up to the surface. As soon as he reached the surface, the broom turned into the dragon's beautiful daughter. Xiong Pao married the princess dragon and lived with his sister and brother-in-law.▼

The Woodcutter, His Rooster and His Wife

A man and his wife lived in a little house, and they were poor. They didn't have any money. The only thing they had was one rooster. The man loved the rooster very much. Every morning when he went to cut wood he always stopped to check on his rooster. Every evening when he came home, he stopped and checked on his rooster again.

One morning the man went to cut wood. He stopped and checked his rooster, then he went to work. His wife stayed home. She swept and cleaned the house. Then she saw someone at the door. It was someone with beautiful clothes. It was the king. He had come for a visit and was going to stay for a while. The wife was surprised and happy. She told him to come in and sit down.

But she was worried. She said, "What can I give the king to eat? I don't have anything. I only have my husband's rooster."

Well, she killed the rooster, and cooked it for the king. The king said, "Very good, very good!"

That evening the woodcutter came home. He went first to the chicken coupe, but didn't see his rooster. He looked everywhere. The woodcutter went into the kitchen and asked his wife where his rooster was. She didn't answer. He became angry and hit her.

The wife began to cry, and the king heard this. He asked her why she was crying. The wife answered, "My husband is angry because I only cooked you a small dinner. I didn't cook you a pig. Instead, I just cooked you a chicken."

The king smiled. He said, "You and your husband are very nice. Even though you don't have any money, you were very polite. I will give you some gold and some silver. You will not be poor anymore. You will be rich."

So the king gave gold and silver to the woodcutter and his wife. They were happy for many, many years afterward. ▼

■ *Pa ndau courtesy of the Science Museum of Minnesota.*

29

The monkeys and the grasshoppers

Illustration by Doua Chang

One day the monkeys went to the grasshopper hill. The monkeys accused the grasshoppers of killing their cousins. The grasshoppers denied the accusation, but the monkeys insisted they did. They decided to fight it out with the grasshoppers. The grasshoppers said, "It is too early to fight. You will have to wait a while until the sun comes up and warms us first."

So the monkeys waited until the sun came up. When the grasshoppers got warm, they jumped on the monkeys' heads. The monkeys got very angry and each got a big stick to kill the grasshoppers. They swung the sticks very hard but couldn't kill the grasshoppers because they jumped away. Instead, the monkeys hit each other's heads. One monkey died. Two monkeys died. Then three, and four and five, and so on.

One of the big monkeys looked around and said, "What happened?" He didn't know why all the other monkeys died and he was the only one left. Then he started eating the grasshoppers one by one. He ate and ate grasshoppers until he couldn't eat anymore, and then he died. ▼

Religion

Shamanism

By Bruce Xiang

My family's religion is shamanism. We still hold on to this religion. My great-great-grandfather brought it from Mongolia. That was the home of shamanism. This religion is still being practiced in China by some of our people there. They have kept shamanism alive for many thousands of years. The Chinese conquered us at one point, but we still kept our religion.

It is important now, in America, to keep shamanism alive. When my parents pass away, the religion will be passed down to me. I get sick just like my father did when he was about to become a shaman. So I think that I, too, must be called to be a shaman. In every way I am able, I will always remember my ancestors and shamanism.

Christianity and Hmong religion

By Shu Yang

To be a Hmong Christian in America is not easy. You get criticized and destructive rumors spread. Since many Hmong people are still Shamanists, there is a lot of opposition to the Christian church.

But Christianity and Hmong religion aren't so different. Biblical characters are similar to Hmong story characters. Take God, for instance. Hmong people have a character in a story like him (Yawm Saub), for which the devil (Dab Ntxwg Nyoos) is the enemy.

As Hmong people become educated and more civilized, most of them will probably become Christians and forget about their culture. As for those who try to stick with their religion and carry on the traditions, they will eventually evolve. But as long as there are still Hmong people living in Laos and Thailand, the Hmong will have hope of avoiding total cultural extinction. ▼

■ *Many Hmong hold fast to animism and ancestor worship. The shaman, or spirit healer (above, center) enters the spirit world in a trance, and attempts to bring back and cure the sick spirit of a person. Other Hmong have converted to Christianity. (Pa ndau photo courtesy of the Science Museum of Minnesota)*

Kao Vang

■ *Kao is a high school freshman and Senior Patrol Leader of Boy Scout Troop 100 for 1993-94.*

Photo by Dan Hess

Kao Vang interviewed his grandmother on his mother's side (Ia Yang, born in 1925). She gave her account of a shaman's calling and special duties.

A shaman's perspective

I became a shaman to cure boys and girls after a couple times when I had been sick and almost died. I started shaking and felt the spirits directing me to be a shaman. This is when the spirits of the shaman will tell you how to cure the people of the land.

The spirits picked me to become a shaman because this role had been passed down through generations in my family. My mother and grandmother both had the shaman calling. They were destined to help cure the clan, to go help the people who needed their help.

If a person is very ill, the shaman will do a traditional ritual. But if the person is not very sick, then the shaman will just tie some white spirit strings to them and sacrifice a

■ *Pictured at right is a collection of some of the "tools" used by a shaman during ritual ceremonies. Counter-clockwise from the cloth pouch are a gong and mallet, a "tambourine," "buffalo horns" used in divining and a pair of finger rattles. (Photo courtesy of the Science Museum of Minnesota)*

32

pig or cow. When shamans perform the traditional ritual, they enter the spirit world to find the sick person's spirit. There they can see what the person's spirit is doing to cause the sickness. If the spirit wants to be sick, then the shaman begs it to allow the person's body to eat again and grow strong and healthy.

The shaman must then sacrifice an animal to plug up the "hole of sickness," a spot that the sick person had carried with him since birth and the place where his spirit was now sleeping.

After the hole of sickness is plugged up with a sacrificed animal, the shaman acts to protect the sick person's spirit. The shaman tells the sick person's spirit not to wander anymore and then proceeds to lock it up. It's as if the shaman were putting a gate around the sick person's spirit. When the spirit is locked up, the shaman says some words to it so it will not run away. The sick person's spirit is then renewed and replaced by a lively spirit. Two other spirits, one male and one female, help the shaman with this renewal.

Returning from the spirit world, the shaman demands that the sick person's illness be cured in a certain amount of time. If the person recovers, the shaman will sacrifice accordingly. If the illness persists, it may be that the sick person's spirit got lost trying to reincarnate into another form. It could be out following different people around. The shaman has another pair of male and female spirits who pass judgments on how and where spirits will reincarnate if a sick person should die. If an illness persists, the shaman will talk with these spirits about how to bring the sick person's spirit back .

> *During the trance, I'm on a shaman's horse into the spirit world. Before I go into a trance, I go through a ceremony where I take out my shaman horse, mount it, and go on my journey. When I return from the spirit world, I dismount . . . and lock up my horse. A shaman's horse is a red horse*
>
> *– Ia Yang*

Spirits taught me the chants and spiritual lyrics. Because my ancestors have always carried the tradition of shamanism, the shaman spirits came to me when I was very young. I was sick in all kinds of ways, but didn't know why. I can remember having bad dreams about climbing very high mountains and then falling off.

The sickness stayed with me. Less than a year after my marriage, I got very sick again with fevers every day. Medicines didn't have any effect.

I got very sick one season while planting corn. My hands and feet got numb and I became unconscious. My husband had to carry me from the corn field to our house, where he sat me by a fire. I started to shake uncontrollably. Being a shaman, my husband put me in front of his altar to see if I would respond to the shaman spirits. My

33

husband set up a special altar for me, and I went into a couple of trances – but I was still sick.

One time, as I stepped out to feed the pigs, I felt a sudden pain in my heart like someone was driving a knife into it. I thought I was going to die. Then, I took off all my clothes because I was sweating to death. A Laotian man in the village who knew magic came over, took four stones out of my body and left. A few minutes later my pain began again, and the Laotian man was summoned back. He removed another four or five more stones from my body, but it didn't help. I thought I was going to die for sure. Then one night I went into a deep trance in front of my altar. This was when I became a shaman.

We learn traditions fromour ancestors, and we want our children to learn them and keep them alive. Keep them alive, and I know that you will prosper. I'm old now, but I'm happy that I've told this to all of my children. ▼

A shaman's tools

The equipment for a shaman's ceremony includes:

■ *The gong*— To help mount the shaman horse.
■ *The shaman sword*— To fight and scare off demons.
■ *Two finger rattles*— To scare off demons.

The shaman tradition

An interview with grandmother Mao Vue by Pang Xiong

I was born in June of 1976. A few years later, my grandpa passed away. He and his parents were the shamans in our family. Several years after, the shaman spirit came to my uncle. This was how it happened:

Thirteen days after his son died, my uncle fainted for ten days and ten nights. This was when the powerful spirits of my grandpa were passed on to him. One of my cousins who lived close to my uncle came over to perform a ceremony, after which my uncle came back to life. He didn't remember anything. He had even forgotten that his son died. My uncle then became a shaman.

Sometime after becoming a shaman, my uncle developed a goiter on his neck. This goiter was because of the kind of spirits he dealt with as a shaman.

A shaman can visit or talk to people who passed away long ago. They do this in ceremonies that can take away illness and make a sick person healthy.

It is said that anyone who gets the sickness when they are four or five years old will become a shaman in the future. In ceremonies, the shaman may order animals to be sacrificed as ransom to the spirits that caused a person to be sick. In many cases, the person's spirit is restored to full health.▼

Funerals as celebrations

By Yee Chang

My friend Dave and I caught a ride with a retired Catholic priest visiting a Hmong village in the National Parks of Northern Thailand. He had received news that a prominant clan leader had passed away and a great funeral was to be held.

In the three days to follow, I journeyed to witness a traditional Hmong funeral and to discover a society far removed from the rest of the world, yet very close to home. I learned to appreciate the way in which the Hmong celebrated life.

The endless, winding highway continued upward over a rocky mountain ridge and disappeared behind a thick cluster of bamboo and shaggy trees. Through the passenger window, I traced the road's path as it reappeared every so often among the blue ridges, around hanging slopes, and onto the next mountain. Below us stretched more mountains and valleys, with streaks of clouds looming over the high tree tops. We had been on the road for four hours when our Toyota pick-up made a turn onto a bumpy, and almost unrecognizable, gravel path.

Thick thorn brushes lined both sides of the path like wire army fences, blocking any view beyond several feet. The next two hours proved to be the ultimate test for our little truck, the driving skill of the priest, and my ability to hold onto my seat. The rocky terrain poked and scratched at the bottom of our vehicle. More than once, I

thought the machine would go helplessly belly-up like a turtle.

What seemed to be an endless journey up, down, and around the thick green mountains ended where the road merged into an open space teeming with brown thatched bamboo huts.

"Well, here we are!" said the priest as he squeezed out of the driver's seat. My friend and I looked at each other in disbelief: We had finally reached our destination, a Hmong village in the center of a wilderness, called Ah Lia (Red Earth) Village.

A thick, rugged, reddish layer of clay covered the uneven surface of the earth. The high altitude greeted me with a gush of cool air that rushed up my nose and down to my chest.

There was a feeling I could not immediately describe as I looked around and saw how isolated the

■ *A kheng player leads a funeral procession to the main village compound. The procession is called, "Tshwm Tshaav" in Hmong. (Photo by Yee Chang)*

35

At a Hmong funeral in Northern Thailand, ten cows stand ready for slaughter. (Photo by Yee Chang)

village was from the world I knew: the world of four lane highways, electricity, and fast food restaurants. Somehow, the village seemed out of place, being in the middle of a jungle. Yet at the same time, maybe it was where it should be. I was reminded of a village just like it – my village – before the communist came and chased us out. My family's journey took me halfway around the world to the Midwestern United States.

But here I was back in my own Hmong village again, undisturbed as it was by the rest of history – so it seemed for a moment. Streets did not exist in the way we know them in the U.S. They were merely dirt paths running from house to house. There were no telephone or light poles. Houses were simple, built from trees of the forest nearby without blue prints or nails. Thatched grass or split bamboo protected the house from sun and rain. Villagers

had developed a hydro-powered grinder for all to use. They also raised pigs, chickens, and cows.

My contemplation of the place was interrupted when the villagers approached to greet us. I immediately felt welcomed when I heard the familiar Hmong voices I had grown up with as a child.

The sun shone bright on the dark heads of villagers as they gathered around, each extending a handshake with a cheerful "Tua Law," which means welcome.

As we were escorted away from our car and into the headman's house, women and children stole a few glances at these curious foreigners.

Inside the house, talk and smoke filled the air. A funeral drum accompanied by a concert of bamboo pipes directed the attention of faces crowding around for a peek at a gold-plated coffin. As I made my way to the coffin, I could hear the lyrics of traditional Hmong death chants. Women stood behind the coffin with hand-held fans to fend off flies and smoke. Children crowded around, only to get in the way of adults who brushed them aside.

We made our way through a parting wall of people and stood before the coffin. We paid our respects and inched our way outside. I stood still for a second and heard the musical utterings of the drum, bamboo pipes and chants echoing in the mountains beyond.

There was a tall blond man in the crowd. He was an Australian anthropologist who knew the clan leader and had been summoned to take part in this celebration. The clan leader had been in his late fifties, a well respected man, the Australian told us, and it was hard to imagine his tragic death by a motorcycle accident. He had been driving home late one night from another village and lost control of his motorcycle as it plunged off the road.

Our friend the retired Hmong priest had made a few converts in this village and was well known by all the villagers, especially the clan leader. He had come to pray for him. Soon, my friend Dave and I were introduced to everyone that the Hmong priest knew, which was almost everyone in the village. I then realized the meaning and magnitude of this funeral in the coming together of families, friends and total strangers like us. I felt as if we all had been summoned for a special occasion.

The village had a population of only one hundred people, so at least two hundred people were visitors or families and friends who had come from other villages. One of the relatives had come from California with fascinating stories of life in America and a strange piece of equipment called a *camcorder*. The majority of the participants in the funeral were Hmong, but a considerable number of them came from different hill tribes nearby to pay their respects to the dead and celebrate with the living.

In the evening, rice whisky flowed freely among male friends and strangers alike. Card and dice games attracted clustered crowds. The children were curious, pushing their heads through the circle of men crouched over a heap of coins and a game-board cloth. The women were in the background, speaking in low voices among each other. They were rarely seen outside of the houses except on an errand to the local water pump. My friend Dave and I joined a more somber crowd listening to fairy tales and life stories around a campfire. As the stars came out, a peaceful quiet could be sensed between the small human voices coming from around the glowing fire.

Next day, in a small clearing beyond the headman's house, a bustling crowd of at least three hundred had gathered to witness the ceremonial sacrifice of ten cows, whose spirits would guide the clan leader to the Other World. Tightly

37

■ *Hmong funer-*
als usually last
three or four days.

fastened to wooden stakes driven into the ground, the cows waited motionless for their inevitable death. Laughter and shouts filled the air as a representative of the clan leader's family raised the butt of his axe over the first cow in line and with a swift hammering motion, buried it into the skull. The cow collapsed, kicked a few times and died. But it's muscles kept twitching. A burst of shouts roared through the smoke-thickened air, as the spirit of the dead cow was finally released from this world.

The ritual continued until the last cow was hammered dead, then the spectators threw up their arms with more shouts and tossed buckets of water into the air in celebration.

A big feast was prepared from the cow meat and the village gathered to celebrate. There was an abundance of self-served beef stew and rice. Everything the village had, they prepared themselves. They grew their own rice, raised their own livestock, and lived literally by their own hands. There was no local supermarket down the street where they could get some extra silverware, napkins, or a case of pop for the visitors. Nevertheless, everyone shared in the ritual of feasting and sat content by the gigantic fires that were built for this purpose.

I was more than content to have participated in the celebration of the clan leader's life. In this tiny, isolated village in the National Parks of Thailand, I had found a thriving, close-knit community. It was one in which the clan leader held the highest authority. It was important to the Hmong that the spirit of the dead have a proper ceremonial send-off to the Other World where his ancestors awaited.

On the last morning, a sudden weary and almost unwilling feeling seized me while I was packing my clothes into the back of our truck. It was going to be a long journey back down the mountains, back to the familiar world of paved sidewalks, electricity, and shops. It was the knowledge that I would never come back to this desolate village again. But no – there was something warm, comforting, and rich about the way in which these people lived and died, and I will never forget that. They lived independently from the rest of society. They were self-sufficient. There was no outside law dictating the limits of their way of life. They were free to celebrate the passing of a great man in the way their culture had taught them.

A crowd of children followed the smoke left by our truck while some brave ones hung onto the sides and back. As we cleared the village entrance they jumped off one by one and vanished from our sight. ▼

Hmong medicine

M y grandmother said that in the old days, the Hmong used their own medicines to treat their illnesses. It came from plants, animals, flowers, leaves and other things. Examples:

Koua Her

■ *Koua is a Junior at Roosevelt High School in Minneapolis and an Eagle Scout from Troop 100.*

Problem	Plant name	Part used
Muscle stanch (cramps)	Tshuaj Ntxees Leeg	Crush leaves, apply
Cuts/scratches (large)	Hmab Nplaum *(water kind)*	Crush leaves, apply
(small)	Hmab Nplaum *(tree kind)*	Crush leaves, apply
Foot injury	Nrhab Liab	Crush vine, apply
Urinary tract problems	Yas Zoov	Boil root in water, drink water
Kidney stones	Tshuaj Npauj Npaim Dawb	Boil root, drink water
	Txiv Tooj Tsiab	Boil root, drink water
	Txeeb Zeb	Boil root, drink water
Headache	Tshuaj Kua Mis	Warm large leaves, wrap forehead

Plant identification:

Tshuaj Ntxees Leeg — Vine with leaves like wild black cherry and yellow-colored root.

Txiv Tooj Tsiab *(Similar to Redbud)* Moss-type vine growth on trees; has maple-type leaves and nuts.

Hmab Nplaum *(Redbud)* Two kinds: large water lily-type variety; smaller moss-type vine growth on trees.

Tshuaj Npauj Npaim Dawb *(White Butterfly Vine)* Tree vine with leaves like wild crabapple, but longer with white and green color. When wind blows, the leaves flutter like a flock of butterflies.

Yas Zoov *(Mosquito Tree)* A tall tree growing near water in the highlands.

Nrhab Liab A small red creeping vine that grows along the ground near water.

◄ **Txeeb Zeb** Moss-like plant that grows only on rock.

Tshuaj Kua Mis Vine with large liquid-filled leaves and yellow nuts.

Research and drawings by Koua Her

39

House Design

Chua Chang

■ *Chua is a sixth grade student at Wilder Contemporary School in Minneapolis.*

Pictured at right is a traditional Hmong house in Northern Thailand.

My name is Sia Chang. I was born to You Mai Chang and Sai Yang in Namsat, Xieng Khuoang, Laos, on May 15, 1955. I was their first child. I liked living in Laos before the war. I lived in a village of about thirty families. At that time, every family was busy farming every day. There weren't any bad people in the village. While the family worked in the fields, they could leave a child alone at home and not worry that anything would happen.

In Thailand, we were refugees for ten months. We didn't have our own house. Everyone lived in a tiny section of big long buildings. We didn't have enough food and water. Once in a while, we got free food distributed by the United Nations. No one could go out of the

Camp. There was a lot of sickness, so we decided to come to the U.S.A.

In Laos, we built our own houses. We might ask the leader of the village where we could build the house, but for the most part we just built wherever we wanted. There were no laws to tell us that we couldn't. It was our village and we were free.

No one owned the woods or the land. We could go into the forest and cut down any tree or get any other material that we wanted for the house. First you must decide on the length and width of your new house and how you will build it.

The Hmong knife (rag), txuas (a heavier and longer knife with a hook at the end), and axe (taus) are common tools for cutting trees for the house. When we cut down any

Hmong measurements

- *ib dlaaj* = length of both arms when stretched.
- *ib npaab* = distance from shoulder to fingertip.
- *ib laab* = distance from chest to fingertip.
- *ib tshim* = elbow to fingertip.
- *ib kauj ruam* = a step.
- *ib noos* = distance from thumb to forefinger.
- *ib xib* = width of open palm.
- *ib yaag teg* = length along finger segments.
- *ib nti* = finger width.

tree or any bamboo, we must carefully measure it first. Then trim it to a desired shape and cut at the right length. After the pieces are prepared, we leave them right where we cut them down. All of the teenagers and adults in the family help carry the materials from the forest to the village. The materials are then piled by the prepared lot where the house will be built.

When all of the house materials are prepared, the village chief and everyone in the village is notified about the day of construction. On that day, every man and woman will take a day off from their farm and come to help. It might take only a day or two put up a house. After it is put up, the owner might kill a pig for a New House Feast to thank all the villagers.

Though the house can be put up in one or two days, it could take about two or three months to prepare all the materials. Sometimes when materials are scarce, it may take up to one year. The important thing is that everything must be ready beforehand.

The foundation of the house consists of six strong poles, four for the four corners, two between the front and back poles. They are driven deep and straight into the ground for better support. To hold up the roof, three smaller but taller poles are placed in a line in the middle of the house. Two long perpendicular poles are placed on top of the foundation poles and another on roof poles. Good poles could last from five to ten years.

We didn't have nails in Laos, so we used ratten or bamboo string to lash the poles together. In fact, most Hmong houses are built without the use of a single nail. Many smaller poles are needed for the roof. Each side of the roof has at least sixty poles. Each of these poles are set at one and a half yards apart. Half of them are set parallel to each other. The others are lashed perpendicular to them, so that the roof looks like hundreds of squares. Then on top of these squares, we placed carved one by three foot

41

■ *Sia Chang explains how a house is built without nails. (Photo by Dan Hess)*

wooden boards as shingles. Between six hundred and eight hundred shingles are needed for a medium size house. There are pegs on each shingle which hook onto the poles of the roof, and no lashing is needed.

We can choose among many materials for the roof of the house. Much depends on what kinds of material we have near the village. Wood is preferred if it is available and there is enough time. If there were a lot of big trees nearby, then we would make wooden shingles. Otherwise, we sometimes use wild grass, which has long stems and may last a few years. We cut them and lay them in the sun to dry for about a month. The next step is to weave them into sheets about two yards wide. About three hundred to five hundred sheets are needed to cover one house.

Other materials for the roof are bamboo and palm leaves. Bamboo is cut at a yard length, split in half,

and the knots inside the hollowed center are cleared. Then they are laid side by side with one covering the other so rain cannot seep through. Another widely used material for the roof is the palm leaf (nplooj kum yem). It may be the most efficient material for roofing. We weave them into sheets like the grass material. Palm leaf is strong and lasts longer than grass. When we can't find enough palm leaves, we sometimes use ratten leaves.

When covering the roof, always start at the bottom of the roof and work toward the top. Unlike wooden shingles, we use ratten ropes to lash these leaf materials onto the roof poles. Wooden shingles are by far the best and could last five years or more. Other materials such as hay and palm leaf need to be changed every two years. If not, just changing the bamboo or ratten lashings will do.

The wall or siding take up a lot of time. Wood or bamboo are the two most common materials for siding. If wood, big trees will be needed. A lot of manpower will be needed to split the logs into six foot segments, then split them into boards. The boards are thin and usually from one foot to a yard wide.

If there are no big trees nearby then bamboo will do. The bamboo is cut into six foot segments, the height of the walls. Then each segment is cut at different places so when slit in half, it will unroll like a sheet about two feet wide. The split segments are then tied together to create the siding. Sometimes we also use smaller bamboo poles instead, as well as clay mixed with hay.

Hmong houses usually have dirt floors. Depending on the size of the family, the house can be divided into several rooms. If the family has small children, the house will have only one bedroom with two beds. If the family has married sons, there would be one bedroom for each son. Children ten years or older can sleep on their own bed in the parent's bedroom. Every Hmong house has a guest bed in the living room, usually near the main fireplace.

Hmong houses can have many different sizes, shapes, and styles. The head of the household usually decides on the design of his house. This process is easy for the ones who are experienced in building houses. It's hard for someone who hasn't built one. Some people build nice houses to live in while others are content with a roof over their head. However built, the house will accommodate their family, no matter how many people. We liked living in Hmong houses because we built them with our own hands.

Other additions to the house can include porches. Some people like to make wide front porches where they can relax and get fresh air. It is also a place where the ladies can do their needlework. Others prefer not to have porches, so they can just walk in and out of the house.

Two Hmong houses

By Shu Yang

There are two types of Hmong houses in Laos and Thailand: the

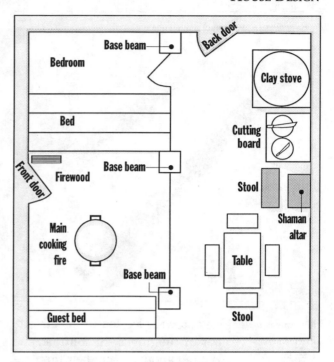

White Hmong and the Green Hmong. They are usually 35 feet long and 20 feet wide. They are made from bamboo, and the roofs are thatched with various materials. Some houses have shingles made from wood instead of grass or palm leaves, and wood siding instead of bamboo. The wood takes longer to prepare but is more durable. The White Hmong house has a side door, whereas the Green Hmong house doesn't. Both houses have a religious altar designed after the specific tradition of the family. The altar is covered with gold and silver paper symbolizing spirit money. The head of the family, the father or the shaman are the only ones who can use the spirit money. It's used as an offering to the spirits of the elders that have passed away.

The Green Hmong house has the fireplace by the front door. Their

■ *The diagram above represents the layout of a typical Hmong house.*

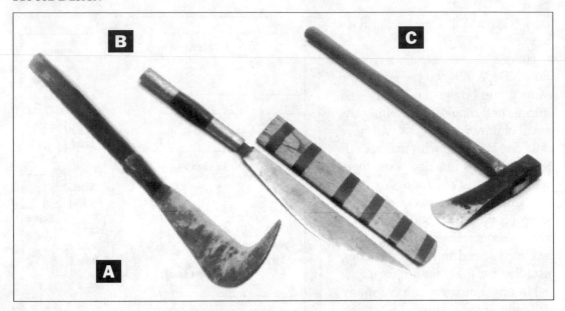

■ *Common tools used in cutting trees for a Hmong house include: A) long hooked knife called a **txuas**, B) a Hmong knife, called a **riam** or **rag**, and C) the axe, or **taus**. (Photos courtesy of the Science Museum of Minnesota)*

clay stove is located in the far corner of the house. In contrast, the White Hmong locate their fireplace and clay stove together in the far corner. Both kinds of house have a cutting board section next to the clay stove. The dinner table is usually low with little wooden stools, which are even lower.

Both have attics to store dry goods such as corn and other seeds for planting. Weapons are stored in the attic too. Attics are prohibited to women and children, maybe for safety's sake. The three main poles or pillars of the house should not be tampered with, especially the center pole. Some are sacred or religious poles (ncej dab, ncej qhua).

Bedrooms commonly take up about an eighth of the house. Wealthy families are be able to build several bedrooms while poor families have one. Wooden porches are also common.

The house has wooden beam-boards and shingles. A common

Hmong knife with a large blade (*riam*, pictured above) is used to cut and notch rafter poles, trim boards, and curve shingle pegs.

A tool called a *txaug* is used to make grooves in the baseboard which anchors the lower part of the wall. It is also used to make holes for pegging beams and doors together.

The *tuam txhob*, a digging tool, is used to clear dirt for the main door frame which is buried two feet into the ground.

The *txuas* (pictured above), a long hooked knife is use to cut small trees and clear a field or site for the building of a new house.

The *piab*, a curved-blade hand adz is used to chip even and smooth wooden surfaces.

The *kuam pav* is used to level the dirt after the holes are dug. The kuam pav is like a mini-bulldozer operated by two people pulling in front and another person pushing with the stick from behind. ▼

Lus Hmoob/Hmong Language

Hmong/English

Peb yuav tsum muab peb cov lus Hmoob khaws tseg. Yog ua le ntawd, peb thiaj li sib txuas lus tau. Peb poob teb poob chaws. Peb tuaj nrog luag coj txuj ci kev cai li cas los muaj. Tshuav peb cov lus Hmoob yog ib yaam uas peb tsi tau muab pov tseg.

Vim tias kuv paub lus Askiv, kuv niam thiab kuv txiv yuav kom kuv pe lus tas li xwb. Kuv yuav tsum ua tus hu xov tooj nrog luag tham thiab pe txhua txhua daim ntaub ntawv. Qhov nov mas tsis yooj yim rau qhov hais tias kuv txhais tsis tau txhua yam rau nkawd. Kuv to taub tias lo lug ntawd hais li cas, tiam si nrhiav tsis tau lo lus uas muaj lub ntsiab xws li. Qhov no yog ib qho ua rau kuv ntxhov siab heev vim tias muaj tej zaum kuv niam kuv ntxiv yuav kom kuv pab los yog kuv xav hais dab tsi rau nkawd, kuv nrhiav tsis tau cov lus lo qhia nkawd li.

Txawm koj paub lus Askiv npaum cas los koj tsis to taub lus Hmoob ces koj yeej pab tsis tau tus ua xav kawm lus Askiv li. Kuv xav tias peb cov tub hluas ntxhais hluas yuav tsum kawm twm, kawm sau, thiab xyaum hais lus Hmoob. Qhov nov yog ib txog kev uas yuav pab tau cov neeg laus.

Kuv pog hais kom txhob hais lus Askiv hauv tsev vim tias ua ntawd ces

It is important that we keep our Hmong language. We need it to communicate with each other. We have lost our country and have taken on many different cultures. One of the only things we have left is our language.

Because I know English, my parents want me to be their translator for everything. They want me to make phone calls, explain every single word in a letter or application. It's tough. I still can't explain everything to them. I understand what it means or what they say, but sometimes I can't find the same word or meaning. It's especially frustrating when I try to describe something that I really want to say or explain to my parents. Sometimes they really need my help, but I just can't find the language to tell them.

It doesn't matter how much English you know. If you can't understand the Hmong language, then you will have a hard time helping the Hmong understand what you are trying to get across in English. I especially think that Hmong teenagers should know, or at least learn how to speak, read, and write Hmong. It is one way to help the older Hmong people.

Pang Xiong

■ *Pang is a senior at Edison High School in Minneapolis.*

Hmong pronounciation guide

■ *Here is a general guide to the pronounciation of Hmong sounds as denoted by letters of the English alphabet:*

Vowels
a = "a" in father
ai = "y" in try
au = "ow" in cow
aw = "ow" on glow
e = "a" in day
i = "e" in we
ia = "ia" in India
o = "o" in lost
u = "ue" in true
ua = "oe" in doer
w = between Hmong "i" and "u"

45

Pronounciation

Consonants

c = "ch" unaspi-
rated
ch = "ch" aspirat-
ed
d = unaspirated
dh = aspirated
f = as English
h = as English
*h_* = indicates
breathy pronoun-
ciation of follow-
ing consonant as
"Hm" in Hmong
k = between Eng-
lish "k" and "g"
kh = English "k"
l = as English
m = as English
n = as English
*n_* = initial n
blending into con-
sonant or conso-
nant cluster as
nplh ("'n p" in
"go 'n play"
p = unaspirated
ph = English "p"
pl = "pl" in ex-
plode
plh = "pl" in play
q = a hard "k",
almost "g"
qh = a softer
Hmong "q"
r = unaspirated,
unrolled
rh = English "r"
s = English "sh"
t = French/Thai
"t", unaspirated
th = English "t"
ts = English "j"
tsh = English "ch"
tx = "ds" in adds
txh = "ts" in cats
v = English "v"
or "w"
x = English "s"
xy = "si" in sign
y = as English
z = as English

kuv yuav tsis nco lus Hmoob lawm. Nyob tim tsev nkawm ntawd ces siv lus Askiv, tiam si kuv yuav tsum xyaum lus Hmoob hauv tsev. Kuv pog hais tias tsev kawm ntawd yog chaws mus kawm lwm yam, es yog peb pheej hais peb cov lus tim tsev kawm ntawv ces peb yuav kawm tsis tau dab tsi li.

Kuv xav tias cov menyuam uas tuaj yug hauv Ameliskas no yuav hais tsis tau lus Hmoob vim tias lawv tsis siv heev los yog tsis tau kawm li. Qhov uas cov niam ntxiv thiab cov menyuam hais tsis tau ib yam lus yog ib qho teeb meem. Ob tog sib nkag siab nyuab. Qhov yuav pab tau mas yog cov menyuam txawj los yog kawm hais lus Hmoob.

Ib txoj hauv kev uas peb yuav khaws tau peb cov lus mas peb yuav tsum siv cov lus ntawd tas mus li xwb. Peb yuav tsum siv thaum peb nrog Hmoob tham. Yuav tsum kawm twm thiab kawm sau ntawv Hmoob peb thiaj tsis hnov qab. Thiab peb yuav tsum qhia peb cov menyuam tib yam li ntawd. Cov coob mas yeej paub hais lus Hmoob lawm, tiam si cov yau mas qho tug thiaj txawj sau thiab twm ntawv Hmoob. Peb cov lus yuav muaj nuj nqi ob peb tiam tom ntej no. ▼

My grandmother tells me not to speak English when I am home because I will forget my native language. I can speak English when I am in school, but I should practice my Hmong when at home. She says that school is a place for us to learn and speak English, and we should not speak our native language in school because then we will learn nothing.

I think that it is much harder for the kids who were born in the U.S. to speak Hmong because they don't speak it as often or have never learned it. It is a problem when the children and parents don't speak the same language. It's hard for the two to understand each other. It would help if the children knew how or learn to speak Hmong.

One way we can keep our language is to keep using it. Use it when we are with Hmong people. Learn how to read and write in Hmong so we won't forget. And teach our children the same. I think many Hmong may know how to speak it, but only few Hmong children know how to read and write it. Our native language will be useful in generations to come. ▼

Tone markings

Final consonants indicate a word's spoken tone and are not pronounced. Words without a final consonant are spoken in a neutral mid-tone. There are eight tones in the Hmong language, represented in English by: no final consonant (neutral mid tone), *-b* (high), *-j* (high falling), *-v* (mid rising), *-g* (breathy mid-low), *-s* (low), *-m* (low falling), and *-d* (low falling and rising).

Music 7

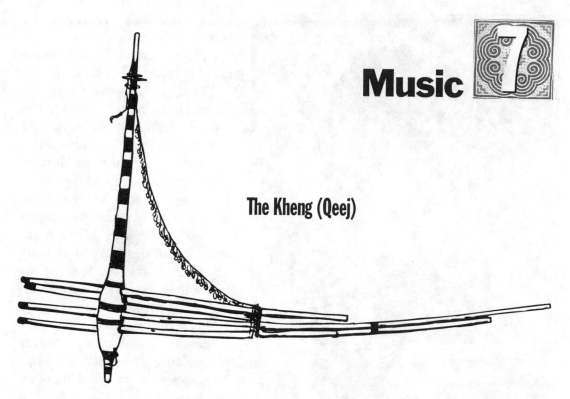

The Kheng (Qeej)

What is the story behind the kheng, and why did I learn it? This is the root or the origin of Kheng. A long time ago, the art of this music was called Zaj Qeeg (kheng of the dragon). Our ancestors learned it from Dragon Land (Zaj Teb) in another dimension, or a place and time before this. Today, our reference to Zaj Qeeg still refers to the dragon whom we first learned it from.

Before you learn how to play the Qeej, you first have to learn the notes or finger movements called ntiv. After you have mastered the tunes of each note, then you will learn more complicated verses.

There is a difference in White Hmong and Green Hmong kheng.

The White Hmong kind takes a longer time to learn the introductory kheng song. Green Hmong usually teach important basics first, like the ntiv. Then, you will learn the introductory song. This introductory song is commonly played at funerals for the dead. Kheng music is generally for the deceased, but there are also songs for other occasions, such as the New Year.

Learning kheng is not easy. It takes a lot of time and patience to become a kheng player (txiv qeej). It takes years, maybe similar to how Americans earn their college degrees.

Kheng music in the land of the dragon was more than just music. It was a powerful way to speak, travel, and fight with spirits. They

Gkao Vang

■ *Gkao is a senior at Edison High School in Minneapolis. He interviewed kheng player (Txiv Qeej) Toom Xais Vaj.*

■ *You Mai Chang dances with the Kheng (dlha qeej). (Photo courtesy of Sai Yang)*

song. Then they decided that it would be better and easier to put the pipes together so one person could play all the positions.

Khengs are different among different Hmong groups who live in different regions. For instance, the Hmong in China play a little different from us. They use the kheng to celebrate in dances and mostly for fun. They play their kheng in "Qeej haiv," a style of sound that people can sing along with. I have heard this kind of qeej played in Long Cheng, Laos. The style is very similar to the Green Hmong's "Qeej Seev," but not like White Hmong's "Qeej Laj or Qeej Xib."

There is a reason why khengs are played during funerals. Long ago, humans were born with skin of tin and bone or metal. People lived to the age of one thousand years. When people were born, they were very little, but they could eat cattle and water buffalos. They ate a lot. They saw that the world was too small to support all of them. So, from that time on, people decided some should die so there would be enough room for others to live. And kheng was used to guide the spirit back to their ancestors after they died. You see, we were part of a large family. ▼

say that kheng music can make you walk through different dimensions, or take you to the heavens and back to earth (mus saum ntuj rov los rau ntiaj teb). The elders say that you are finished learning kheng when you can make flames come out of the bamboo pipes (ntiv qeej) of the instrument.

The kheng is made of six bamboo pipes. There is a reason for the six pipes. A long time ago, there were six brothers, and each of them played a pipe. They played together in an ensemble to make one

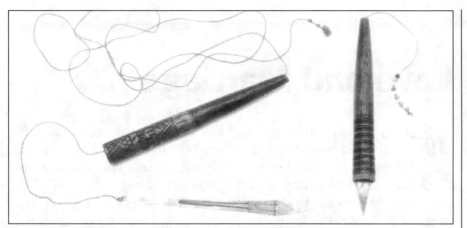

Mouth harp (Ncaas)

Song Ger Thao described a jaw harp, or what we might call a Jew's harp. It seems that every young man or woman who was single used these to talk to each other. For the Hmong, there is not the separation between music and words that we have: the musical sounds themselves stand for words; they *are* words. So the young man would go out at night, tap on the wall of the bamboo or wooden hut where his girlfriend was sleeping, and talk to her by playing the Jew's harp. And she could reply in like manner. If you carried around a Jew's harp tucked into your sash, it was a signal that you were "available."

Leaf blowing

The young don't know much about this kind of music. There is hardly an instrument. It involves a good mouth and a leaf from a plant or tree, almost any leaf.

In the old country, people farmed every day in the fields or mountains. During breaks, or just to pass the time, leaf blowing was a favorite for making good sounds and communicating with a loved one on another distant mountain. The sound of leaf blowing travels far, sometimes over a few mountains. It gets boring sometimes when you're all alone on a mountain. It's not like youths today who can just turn on the radio and listen to music.

Leaf blowing is like the telephone we use today. Sometimes it is the only way to communicate with a friend who farms on another mountain. There is a leaf blowing language that you must know in order to communicate. Different tunes mean different things. So you can talk back and forth through songs played on the leaf.

There are many different ways to intepret the songs. You must understand basic tunes about missing each other, wanting to see each other, etc. Anyone who knows how to blow leaves knows the general tunes and can translate them. It just takes practice to learn how to blow the right tunes. ▼

Love and Marriage

Doua Thao

■ *Doua is a student at Edison High School and member of Boy Scout Troop 100.*

A long time ago there was a couple who were deeply in love. They were Dao Kia and Gao Kia. The young man, Dao Kia, told Gao Kia to stay on Earth while he went to learn new things up in heaven. He would return in three years. He told her to wait for him and when he returned, they would get married.

Gao Kia stayed. She was very sad and lonely. She played the flute and played songs by blowing on leaves. One day she told her mother that she was going to the lake to get some water. She would come back in a little while.

When she got to the lake, she was still very sad. She picked a couple of leaves from a tree and blew on them to make a song. From the bushes, a tiger heard her playing the leaves. The tiger jumped out at her and killed her. He took her away. The tiger took her spirit away and left her body there. Meanwhile, at home, Gao Kia's mother was getting worried about where she could be. She went out out the lake to look for her.

Gao Kia's mother arrived at the lake. She saw that Gao Kia was dead. She cried and cried and cried and took her body home.

Dao Kia would come home from heaven in three days. When he got home, they had already buried Gao Kia. Dao Kia was very sad, so he went out to find her grave. He hid himself in some tall grass near the grave and waited.

He looked at Gao's grave and saw a big black tiger. The tiger came to the grave and blew three breaths at the head of the grave and three breaths at the foot of the grave. The tiger then began to dig up the grave. Gao Kia jumped up from the gave, hopped onto the tiger's back and rode away to be his wife.

Dao Kia came home and told his mother what he had seen. He told her to get his sword ready. He also told her to kill their only pig for him as his lunch because he was going after Gao Kia and the black tiger.

His mother said, "My son, we don't have much and that's the only pig we have. If I kill it for you then we won't have anything."

Dao Kia said, "Mother, if you really love me, you will give me that pig and let me test my sword on it. If I cut it into three pieces in two blows, then I will know that I'm ready to go." His mother gave him the pig and he cut the pig into three pieces in just two blows. So Dao Kia went on his way to get Gao Kia back.

While he was traveling, he came to a mountain covered with itch weed. He couldn't cross, so he took out his bow and a magic red arrow and shot at the itch weed. The itch weed burned down and died, and he crossed.

When he caught up to Gao Kia, the black tiger asked, "What are you doing here, boy?" When the tiger asked that, the girl answered quickly that Dao Kia was her brother and he just missed her a lot because the tiger came and took her away. And he just followed her there. Then Dao Kia went with Gao Kia and the big tiger. They climbed a big cliff, and when they got to the top, they decided to stop and sleep there for the night.

Now below the cliff was a couple of blind tigers, and whatever fell off the cliff they would eat. There were four ghosts with the tigers. At night they arranged for Dao Kia to be at the edge of the cliff so they could push him down to be eaten by the blind tigers. But Gao Kia gave Dao Kia her needles. When the ghosts tried to push him, he could stick them with the needles. Gao Kia knew that the ghosts were going to push Dao Kia over the cliff, so she gave Dao Kia a piece of her clothing and moved him, putting the two ghosts where he was sleeping. When one of the ghosts gave a push, it pushed another ghost down thinking it was Dao Kia.

Then one of the other ghosts got up to see if Dao Kia was still there. Seeing the black figure and thinking it was Dao Kia trying to run away, the black tiger gave a kick at the ghost, who fell down and was eaten too.

In the morning the two remaining ghosts saw that their buddies were gone and that Dao Kia was still with them. They went on traveling further, and Dao Kia could see that Gao Kia had already grown a tail two inches long.

Dao Kia said to Gao Kia, "Gao Kia, tell me where you are going to be, because I'm getting hungry and I'm going to go home. I will come back later."

Gao Kia said, "If you're hungry and you want to go, then you can go." And she told him that the next time he came, they would be up in the mountain in a cave.

When he got home Dao Kia told his mother that he saw Gao Kia and that she should pack a lunch for him because he was going back to get Gao Kia.

His journey back took him seven days to reach the high mountain where Gao Kia lived. All of the tigers were out hunting and there was only Gao Kia sitting at home doing pa ndau. When he got there Gao Kia greeted him. He asked if all the tigers had gone hunting. She said that pretty soon they would come home so he should hide. She told him to hide in a big pot and she would sit on top of him doing her pa ndau.

As the sun was setting, all the tigers started coming home. When the black tiger came, he asked why it smelled like fresh meat in the compound.

"Maybe it was because you just ate it and you just smelled it on

51

■ *Newlyweds wave good bye after three days of feasting and rituals. (Pa ndau photo courtesy of the Science Museum of Minnesota)*

your breath," said Gao Kia. The tigers started sniffing around and came closer and closer to the big pot where she sat. She told the tigers to go and kill a pig for a feast because her brother was coming soon. All of the tigers left except for Gao Kia's two little cubs.

When Dao Kia came out, the two little tigers tried to eat him, so he killed them both. He cut their heads off and stuck them on two sticks. Then he climbed a tree to wait for the rest of the tigers. The first tiger (grandpa tiger) came back and saw the two dead tiger cubs. He was furious that his grandsons were dead. He looked around to see who did it. He looked up into the tree and saw Gao Kia. The tiger jumped up three times to get him but couldn't.

Then Dao Kia said, "Tiger, if you're long I'll cut you into three pieces and if you're short I'll cut you into two pieces." So when the tiger jumped up, he swung his sword twice and the tiger was in three pieces.

After a while a second tiger came. He was as big as five humans combined and his teeth were one foot long. He saw that his grandpa was dead so he was very angry. He looked around and saw Dao Kia. And the tiger said to Dao Kia, "Are you going to come down or do you want me to come up?"

"If you want to come up, you can," said Dao Kia. So the tiger climbed up and got his head chopped off. When the rest of the tigers came and saw what had happened, they all got really scared and ran off. Then Dao Kia took Gao Kia away.

Three years after they had returned home, a ghost appeared to to take Gao Kia back to the tigers. When Gao Kia kept getting sick, Dao Kia looked out the window and discovered the little white ghost sitting on a rock. It had cast a spell on Gao Kia to make her sick.

The little ghost came there every night. Knowing this, Dao Kia took the rock and burned it until it became red hot. Then he set the rock back where it had been. When it got dark, the ghost came back and sat on the rock. He got burned so badly that he never came back again. ▼

The moral of this story is if you have true love then wherever your lover goes, there you'll go and find her so you guys could be together again.

Ways of Hmong Marriage

Mai See Xiong

■ *Mai See is an eighth grade student at Folwell Jr. High School in Minneapolis.*

Before I say something about Hmong marriage, I would like to introduce myself. My name is Chia Ye Xiong. I became a soldier when I was 13 years old and fought in many battles. After May 5th, 1975, when we lost our country to the Communists, I joined the resistance movement called Chao Fa until October 9th, 1979. After that, I escaped to Thailand. The trip took four months, but we finally made it to Refugee Camp Ban Vinai. Because of all those years as a soldier, I now have many kinds of illnesses.

This is what I know and experienced about traditional Hmong marriages.

For us Hmong people, if a young man reaches the age of 15 to 20 years old, he will likely be married. Before he marries, however, he must choose a suitable family. For example, a family that is well to do, affluent or involved in politics. The young man must be patient. He must ask the young girl if she likes him enough to marry him. In this case, he must get to know her and can then marry her when she agrees.

Three types of marriages.

The first kind is when the young man and the young woman like each other and agree to marry one another. They must tell each other that they plan to get married. They must understand each other and promise to love each other to the end. Essentially, the young woman has decided to run away with the young man.

The young man must let his parents know of his intentions. The reason for doing so is that the parents will pay the bride price. They have to take care and plan the marriage ceremonies. Then they will invite relatives and leaders of the clan to attend the wedding.

If a young man does not tell his parents and relatives about his plans for marriage, he will not get support from them.

In the recent past, we often wore Laotian clothes or Western clothes when we get married. But, traditionally, we must wear our Hmong clothes. After all, we are Hmong. If we wear other clothing for this occasion, we somehow lose a part of ourselves.

When the young man is ready to get married, he must find two more people to go with him, so that when they bring home the new bride, there will be four of them. It is important to have even numbers of people going, mostly for good luck.

When they get back home with the bride, the parents will be waiting for them. The married couple's

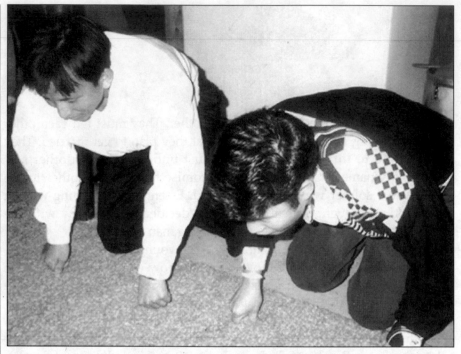

■ *The groom, Charlie Chang, and his "Phij Laaj" (best man) Ya Chang must kneel before each of the bride's relatives to pay respect and receive blessings. (Chang family photo)*

company must wait by the door. The father or older brother of the family will first take a chicken and bless the house to rid it of bad spirits. After this ceremony, the new bride can come in by herself, or the groom will pull her inside the house.

In Laos, the bride will come in the house and stand in front facing the main door. But in this country, she can stand anywhere. She must not sit down yet. First, the groom and his company of family negotiators or representatives (txiv tuam mej koob) and best man (phij laaj) must kneel before the parents, relatives, and household and ancestral spirits. After the kneeling, the mother or her daughter-in-laws will invite the bride to sit down.

The second type of marriage is when the young woman's parents don't want her to get married yet. In most cases, these young women do not favor the idea of chasing after a husband. They listen to their parents about not running away. They would rather have the young man come and propose. So, the parents must give prior consent. In this case, the young man must go to the woman's house with two chosen negotiators/representatives and a best man and ask her parents to give her away.

The family representative is the leader of the groom's party. He must bring with him an umbrella tied with a special woman's head strap. These two items will immediately indicate the group's purpose: a wedding proposal.

When they arrive at the young woman's house, they must first kneel before her parents, then relatives and household and ancestral spirits. Then, the family representa-

■ *The bride price negotiation involves two representatives (mej koob) from each side of the family. (Chang family photo)*

tive will offer the parents cigarettes and confirm that they intend to marry their daughter. He also offers to help them summon their relatives and clan leaders to join in the discussion.

When they arrive, they ask the young woman whether she wants to marry the young man who had proposed. They may not want her to get married either and should tell her then. In case they don't agree to give her away, then the young man's company must offer some money to overcome the reluctance. This money is given directly to the young woman's parents. The parents usually get one silver bar each; older and younger brothers and aunts and uncles get an equal amount of cash. A person from the young woman's side is chosen to represent her family, and he is also

given some money.

By this time, the family might agree to marry their daughter off, in which case a date will be decided for the official wedding. Both sides decide how the wedding will be arranged. In this case, where the young man came and proposed, the young woman's family will have to provide some chicken and a sizeable pig for the wedding. At this point in the discussion, the dowry money for the bride can be paid to her family.

If the young woman's family or relatives are well to do, she will receive many gifts. Some of the gifts will include silver bars, skirts, blouses, silver necklaces, pa ndau works, and many other silver jewelry. They would also promise to kill a cow for the couple on their first visit back.

At the end of the wedding, the

will bring two or three other people to help him win the young woman over. If they can force her to come home with them, then they need to find two people to send a message to her parents to tell them what happened. The messengers must tell the parents exactly what happened, for them not to worry, and that their daughter was taken by such and such clan for a wife. They must assure the young woman's parents that she is safe somewhere. The messengers must also present to the parents some cash tied up in the special women's head strap.

The parents may or may not agree to the forced marriage, depending on whether or not they accept the money. Regardless of the decision, the messengers must kneel to them, the rest of their relatives and household and ancestral spirits. The messengers will also offer the parents cigarettes and ask them to find two representatives for a negotiation of the marriage.

After the work of the messengers, the young man must find his representatives, the best man, and a girl from his own clan to accompany the bride and go back for the negotiation. But before they leave, the young man's family will do a ceremony to bless the bride-to-be and son by tying strings around their wrists. On their way, they must bring with them five chickens; two to be eaten for lunch, two to give to the two representatives after the negotiation, and one for the spirits. They also bring with them an umbrella, a apron, two red waist sash-

family will toast farewell drinks to the groom's company as they leave. They also give them four cooked chickens for their journey back. The groom and his company give thanks to the parents and return home. On the way, they usually stop to rest and eat. Two chickens are normally eaten for lunch. Two are saved for the young man's parents and the spirits that reside in the bride's new home.

The third type of marriage is when the young woman is not interested in the young man, but the young man insists on marrying her. Maybe the young woman has many talents, or she comes from a well to do family, and his family will gain much from the marriage. In any case, the young man must try to win her over. One way is to give her things and see if she accepts. If she does, then he can claim that her action was a signal to marry him.

In cases like this, the young man

56

es, one of which is tied to the umbrella.

The umbrella has been used as a tool to represent marriage because it is said to protect the newlyweds and contain all the good fortunes their new life will bring. It has been passed down many generations to us. When the groom's company arrives at his in-law's house, the representative hangs the umbrella on the high beam of their house. After the negotiation, the representatives from both sides take turns holding the umbrella and sing to each other the commitments each family will make. Near the end, the umbrella is used to direct the groom and best man in kneeling to pay respect and receive blessing from the bride's family and relatives.

On their way back home, the groom's company will stop for lunch again and have chicken.

When they get home, they kneel before the parents, family, relatives and spirits and pay respect.

So those are the different ways one can get married. Usually after one year, especially if they have given birth to a child, they will visit their in-laws. The in-laws then usually kill a pig for them and bless them in a ceremony.

After a young man has two or more children, he will be given a different name, to mark his transition from young man to fatherhood.

This is what I know about Hmong marriages. ▼

Kidnapping brides considered old tradition

According to respected Thao clan elder Song Ger Thao, the more cosmopolitan Hmong of Nong Het near the Lao-Vietnam border had a reputation for kidnapping brides. Song Ger said that the more isolated, traditional Hmong of Xieng Khouang province in the interior of Laos had never adopted this practice, and that General Vang Pao, the Hmong military chief, had put an end to it. Song Ger was glad for this.

An unmarried young man would be regarded as a boy, even if he had reached the age of adulthood. Until he married, it would be an elder's role to instruct the boy and keep him in line for the good of the clan. Song Ger disparaged the practice of kidnapping a bride, especially in America, because it could only bring shame and pain upon the whole clan.

Pa Ndau/Costumes

Tong Thao

■ *Tong is a senior at South High School in Minneapolis and an Eagle Scout of Boy Scout Troop 100.*

One of the most important things that the Hmong People carry with them wherever they go is their traditional art of *pa ndau*, or embroidered fabric, which helps keep their culture and values alive for future generations. In most cases, their cultures were lost. But the Hmong people found out a way to preserve their culture.

Through pa ndau, the Hmong people were able to maintain their traditional culture and values. There are many complex symbols in pa ndau that represent the Hmong and their culture. The Chinese could not understand the symbols hidden in the pa ndau, and thought that it was only art work. Many Hmong say that pa ndau was once used as a communication tool because the Chinese prohibited the Hmong from using their language. pa ndau was the only way for Hmong to relay messages to one another. Clearly, for the Hmong, pa ndau was a way to express and celebrate their culture in a society where it was forbidden.

After a failed uprising against the Chinese, the Hmong fled south into the modern countries of Laos, Vietnam, and Thailand. They took with them the art of pa ndau. And everywhere they went, it was the one thing that identified them as Hmong.

Two types of pa ndau

Pa ndau, which literally means "flower cloth" has many patterns and designs. There are two types of pa ndau. The first consists of pictures, designs and patterns, while the other consist of only designs and patterns.

The first type of pa ndau, also know as "story cloth," interprets and depicts folklore, children's stories, animal stories, legends, and many other kinds of stories. The story is at the center space of the pa ndau while the designs and patterns are around the edge. One fa-

■ *example of a story cloth.*

58

mous pa ndau story was based on the Hmong exodus from Laos to Thailand. It depicted people crossing the Mekong River and Communist soldiers chasing them from behind. Another famous Pa ndau story was one about a tiger that ate up a family one by one until the youngest daughter found a way to stop him. In the end, she killed the tiger. This story varies among different storytellers in the Hmong community. Sometimes the son in the family is the last survivor.

These story-telling pa ndau are usually fashioned in square shapes of different sizes. They can be found hanging on a living room wall, as an apron or blanket and other decor. The designs around the Pa ndau are made of small multicolored triangles, lines, swirls or circles. These forms are used to represent mountains, hills, valleys, rivers, or corners of a house. In recent years, story lines in English have been sewn onto pa ndau so Americans can understand what is going on in the art work. All the designs and patterns, and objects such as animals, plants and people are hand sewn. This type of pa ndau is usually made from cotton.

The second type of pa ndau is more of the traditional art. It consists of only designs and patterns. The difference between this kind and the "story cloth" is that it is a foundation for all Hmong costumes. The pa ndau (embroidered cloth) could be used as a part of a blouse, a sash, skirt, hat, baby carrier, etc. Depending on whether a

■ *Two examples of a traditional design pa ndau. The pattern above represents the work of a White Hmong artist.*

person is Green, White, or Stripe Hmong, the pa ndau on their costumes are worn differently and have different designs. There are more than seven varied costumes among Hmong women. And they are different in colors, designs, and patterns. Though they are different costumes in terms of design and wear, they share a basic Hmong characteristic, pa ndau. From bottom to top, the Hmong woman's costume may consist of leg wrap-

59

pings, pleated skirt, front apron, the first sash, shirt, the second sash, necklace and turban or hat. Another kind of costume may include loose pants, two sashes, shirt and turban.

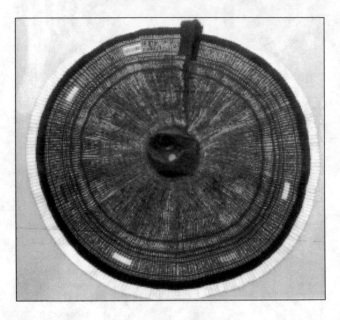

■ *Green/Blue Hmong skirt. (Photo courtesy of the Science Museum of Minnesota)*

The Hmong skirt

The skirt is made from a pleated (multicolored for Green Hmong and plain white for White Hmong) rectangular sheet of fabric wrapped around the waist. The skirt is probably the most complex pa ndau and, again, it has many patterns and designs. It could take up to three to four months to finish – sometimes a whole year. In Laos, before the Hmong had access to better cloth, they used Ma (hemp) fiber to make their skirt. The long process of making a Hmong skirt started with taking strips of bark from the Ma plant. They were boiled, washed until white, turned into a yarn, and finally weaved into

cloth. The next step was to make patterns on the skirt in a process called batik, in which designs are made by covering fabric parts with removable wax. A wax pen is used to carefully draw and construct the patterns and designs on the cloth. After completion of design, the cloth, which is usually 10-12 feet long and 3 feet wide, is dipped into hot water and hung out to dry.

The Hmong skirt is still made in this same method. But back in Laos almost the whole costume is made from hemp. Today, Hmong skirts are almost all imported from Laos and Thailand. This complex pa ndau is very important to the Hmong woman. A Hmong elder woman said, "My mother told me that if I wear this skirt when I die, then I'll be able to find her in heaven."

Other parts of a woman's costume

To accompany the beautiful skirt, Hmong women wear various other pieces, such as the apron and blouse with matching pa ndau on them also. On the blouse, the pa ndau are sewn onto the long collars. A special pa ndau is also attached to the blouse as a loose collar on the back of the neck. Today, blouses come in modern designs, some even glitter. Some are done with sewing machine, but most of the pa ndau part are still done by hand. A couple of sashes (usually one red and one green) are wrapped around the waist and the ends are left hanging on the back. More common in Laos than in the

PA NDAU/COSTUMES

U.S., Hmong women also wear leggings. These are long strips of a black cloth wrapped around the leg from the ankle to the knee.

Depending on the type of Hmong group a person comes from, she will wear a hat or various types of turbans. The White and Green Hmong women may wear a long stripe of black cloth wrapped around their head in an orderly pattern. A smaller strip of checkered cloth is wrapped in the shape of an "x" over the turban. They may also wear a rectangular shaped hat, with three angles pointing upward, like mountains or hills. This type of hat has many pa ndau designs and is very colorful. The Stripe Hmong wear a cylindrical hat that has red furry cloth balls

hanging around it. It is also very colorful.

Finally, after all these pieces are put on, it is time for the jewelry. An intricate silver necklace, weighing two pounds, is worn around the neck. Other jewelery includes coin sashes worn around the waist, and coin bags worn criss-crossed over the shoulders. These sashes are heavily and intricately designed with pa ndau.

Mens' costumes

In general, the Hmong woman's costume bears the most pa ndau. Though it is true that the men's costumes are more plain, they are different in other ways. The shirt and pants are usually black. A bright

61

■ Pictured at right are (from top to bottom) a baby carrier, several varieties of Hmong hats, a Green/Blue Hmong shirt, bracelets and a variety of silver earrings. (Photos courtesy of the Science Museum of Minnesota)

red sash is wrapped around the waist, with the ends hanging down in front. A plain black hat with a red knot on top is common, but there are also pa ndau hats with color cloth balls on top. The main difference between White Hmong and Green Hmong in the men's wear is their pants. The Green Hmong's pants are baggy and loose, while the White Hmong's are pajama-like. Stripe Hmong also have a patch of pa ndau on the back of the shirt. The most colorful costumes for Hmong men are from the regions in northern Thailand. Pa ndau cover their whole outfit.

There are many different kinds of Hmong with different costumes, but the most common are worn by the White, Green, Stripe, and Chinese Hmong. The costume parts of two different types of Hmong should not be mixed. For example, a White Hmong hat with a Stripe Hmong skirt. In Laos, one could generally tell who was White, Green, etc, just by what they wear. Especially during the New Year celebration, bright and colorful costumes are worn. Often times, the costume you wear should say a lot about you; what type of Hmong you are (different dialect), whether you come from a rich family (if you wear a lot of silver), etc.

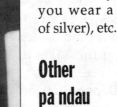

Other pa ndau

Another well known piece of pa ndau is the baby carrier. It is rectangular shaped with two straps of cloth sewn at two corners. The pa ndau work is usually a maze-like or diamond-shaped design centered on the outside of the baby carrier.

The baby is put between the mother's back, and the baby carrier

is wrapped around the baby with the straps over the shoulder from the back, criss-crossed at the chest and around the sides of the waist to the back, tying the baby and again to the front with a final knot.

Another important piece of pa ndau is used when a girl gets married. The mother gives this pa ndau to her daughter and son-in-law as a going-away present. The daughter and her husband give thanks to their parents by butchering a pig for a feast. The parents of the son-in-law also give one of these pa ndau to the mother of the daughter in return. This pa ndau is called, Noob Ncoo (Nong Jong). The designs and patterns are concentrated on a square shaped cloth, with distinct features and colors designed for the occasion of marriage. ▼

Pa ndau: a learned art

Mothers taught pa ndau to their daughters at a very young age. Boys are taught different skills, such as hunting, by their father. Because pa ndau takes a long time to learn, one must start early, sometimes as early as 5 or 6 years old. It takes a lot patience, concentration, time and skills. It also takes good eyes and steady hands. For these reasons and some taboos, a few boys do pa ndau.

pa ndau is art. It is learning how to make designs on clothes, create stories of past events, keeping the Hmong culture alive. Someone in the family should know the skill. Otherwise, they would have to buy it from others. And others make their pa ndau that represent them. A person who knows pa ndau looks hard for the right one. However learned, it is important to keep our Hmong tradition alive so that younger generations will know

■ *Pictured above are examples of pandow characteristic of (left to right) Stripe Hmong, Green/Blue Hmong and Chinese Hmong. (The first two photos were taken at a Hmong New Year celebration in Fresno, California, by Yee Chang. The last photo was taken at the Hmong New Year in St. Paul, Minnesota, by Dan Hess.)*

63

■ *Above and right, woman in Camp Ban Vinai, Thailand, and young girl in Northern Thailand practices the fine art of pa ndau. (Photos by Yee Chang)*

their past use it as a tool for telling stories.

Because the Hmong are living in many parts of the world now, many more varieties of Hmong costumes are appearing as a result of change. But no matter how many different costumes there are, pa ndau will still be an important element of what it means to be Hmong. This art is something that will always remain with us wherever we go. One day when the old Hmong ways are gone, our children and our children's children will have that trace of pa ndau on their clothes, and they will know that they are Hmong. ▼

64

New Year Celebration

Alee Chang

■ *Alee is a freshman at South High School in Minneapolis.*

Pictured at left is a courtship game of catch called "pov pob." (Photo taken in California by Yee Chang)

My name is Sia Chang. I am thirty nine years old. I was born in Ban Nam Sath, Xieng Khouang, Laos. After leaving Laos, I lived in Ban Vinai refugee camp in Thailand for about ten months. I have been living in the United States for fourteen years.

Our Hmong New Year celebration in Laos is different from the Hmong New Year in the United States.

In Laos, our Hmong people usually celebrate the Hmong New Year at about the end of November each year. This is just after the harvest season. The crops have all been collected. Each family has to prepare for the New Year (Tsab Peb Caug).

This is the only break time for the Hmong during the year. The family has to collect a lot of dry wood for the fireplace. The women have to sew new clothes for the family. Every family has to prepare Hmong whiskey, rice cakes, and lots of rice.

On the early morning of the 30th day of the 12th month of the Buddhist calendar, one person from each family has to go to the rice or corn fields to call the family spirits home for the new year. He or she takes an egg with three burning sticks of incense and carries an empty backpack. When the person arrives at the field, he or she grabs some left-over rice or corn, puts it into the backpack, and says,"ib xyoo kaum ob lub hlis, xyoo laug

65

■ Once a year, young men and women, boys and girls of all ages, participate in a traditional courtship game. A ball is tossed between pairs, and each miss results in the surrender of some personal item or favor. Favors may include singing a song. This game, called Pov Pob (Paw-Pa) in Hmong, is a good way for people to meet and have fun. (Pa ndau photo courtesy of the Science Museum of Minnesota)

taag, xyoo tshab tuaj, nub nua peb yuav noj peb caug , kuv tuaj hu mej plig qoob plig loo suav dlawg nrug kuv moog noj peb caug." (Translation: One year round. There's twelve months. The old year has passed. Tomorrow will be a new year. I am here to call all the spirits home with me to have the New Year's party.) Then he or she goes back home. Each family must have an elder in the village to help call the spirits home for the new year (hu plig noj peb cuag). To do this, we use an egg for each person, two chickens (one male and one female) for the family spirit, one chicken for crops, money, and the animal's spirit, and one rooster for the house's spirit. We usually invite some older people in the village to join the party. This is not a big feast. But for the big feast (noj tsab) we can have it before or after the new year's day. This is when we invite a lot of the people to join in. The feast is set up by the villagers.

On New Year's eve, everybody has to take a bath to wash every bad thing away along with the old

year. Everybody should have a clean body for the new year. All of the household owners have a get-together. They want to know which animal will make the first cry. If they hear no animal except the rooster then it means that the year will go well without any problems. No bad things will happen in the village through the year.

On the first day of the celebration, everyone gets up very early. After breakfast, the mother gives everyone new clothes which she has made or sometimes purchased. In addition, everyone wears jewelry for the special occasion. This is the moment everyone has been waiting for. People cannot spend any money on the first day of the year.

The young people head towards the ball-tossing field which is chosen by the village leaders. Usually the festival occurs at the village where the big feast is held. It's a time for the young people to meet each other and make new friends. They also throw balls. No one can refuse an offer to play ball. Boys and girls throw to each other. Sometimes a girl may throw with more than one guy or vice-versa. They get to know each other as they throw the ball back and forth, and by singing (lug txaj) a traditional song. In that way many couples fall in love and get married shortly after. The younger children also throw balls. While that goes on, the elders watch the children play, watch bull fights, water-buffalo fights, horse races, or play games with tops. The celebration generally lasts for about ten days, but this depends upon whether all the work has been done. If the harvesting is not finished, the celebration will be cut short so people can return to work.

Many things changed for the Hmong people when we came to the U.S. The New Year festival has changed too. The event now depends upon the American calendar. The celebration is held in Minnesota toward the end of November.

In Laos, the moon and the Buddhist calendar set the time for everyone. The calling of the spirits would happen on the exact same day for all families. In the U.S. this usually happens during the same week. The spirit calling is not done by approximately one-fourth of the American Hmong population, although some of these may attend a relative's ceremony. The anticipation of the New Year is felt more strongly among the Hmong in Laos than here.

The young Hmong in the U.S. have many more opportunities to meet and talk. The New Year is just one more. In Laos, people are so busy with all the work that they have no time to see each other. So the New Year is a really big occasion to get together.

In Minnesota, a stage has taken over the primary place at the New Year. Also, the cold of Minnesota weather has forced everyone indoors. Instead of ball-tossing or other games that still go on here, many people just watch the dances, beauty contests, modern singing, etc. Many young people no longer know the words of the traditional Hmong songs. The forms of the songs are complex, like a rhyming couplet, and the youngsters are not able to improvise as their parents did.

The faces of the elders reflect their disappointment when they see that the younger generation is forgetting or rejecting their culture. They walk around wondering about how things have changed.

Even the duration of the New Year celebration has changed. In Minnesota, it lasts just two days, whereas the traditional celebration lasted about ten to fifteen days. The time off from work and the cost of renting the Saint Paul Civic Center have shortened the amount of time available.

The number of feasts in America has also dropped. In Laos, extended families lived together and there was a chance for older people to gather while the younger generation played ball.

Styles at the New Year have also changed. Many of the Hmong clothes and hats now worn by the women were developed in the U.S. People will change out of their traditional clothes after only several hours of wearing them – something that would not happen in Laos, where they wore their New Year clothes all day long.

The old people remember, but the young people forget. ▼

New Year Celebration

A popular attraction at New Year celebrations is the bull fight. Rooster fights, popular all year round, are also held on the New Year.

Courtesy of the Xiong family

Courtesy of Vang Xue Xiong

Courtesy of the Science Museum of Minnesota

Umbrellas at the New Year celebration provide shelter from the hot sun. (Courtesy of Chong Phia Yang)

68

The New Year

■ Clockwise from top, white Hmong girls at New Year Celebration in St. Paul (photo by Dan Hess), Her Lee strikes a pose, girls dressed in white Hmong costume from Sam Neua region (photo by Yee Chang).

■ *Throw the ball, and gain a mate for life. Thousands gather each New Year season, many to find a wife or husband.*

70 *Photos by Yee Chang.*

Xyoo Tshiab

■ *Txiv tuam mej koob — family negotiator Neng Chue Vang inspects dowry money from a bridegroom.*

71

■ *The New Year is a time for people of all ages. At right are "pov pob" participants during Hmong New Year in Fresno, California. The celebration lasted seven days. Picture below are Blia Yao Xiong and Ma Her taken in the '60s in Laos. (Courtesy of Chia Ye Xiong).*

Expectation

❝ . . . *it is a ritual thing to me. But what makes every year a different year is that I do different activities. Like this year I will be in the fashion show and sell things such as jewelry and roses for the Close-Up program to go to Washington, D.C.* **❞**

–May Nhia Yang

❝ . . . *whatever happens happens. Sometimes nobody can stop it. I expect to meet a lot of people, but not . . . a special friend. I hope I will have fun and enjoy the New Year; wear my Hmong costume, hang around or walk around, meet new friends and old friends and take pictures.* **❞**

–Pang Xiong

❝ *Mostly it's just a large group of people walking around talking, entertainment and many. . . activities.* **❞**

–Paul Yang

■ *Hmong elders celebrate the New Year in Fresno, California by engaging in singing traditional songs. Fewer young people today know how to sing Hmong songs or lullabies. Pictured below left is shaman and respected elder of the Yang clan, Nhia Yer Yang at Hmong New Year in St. Paul, Minnesota.*

❝ *Besides meeting people, I don't really expect anything because whatever happens happens.* ❞

–Mai Nhia Xiong

❝ *I just want to have fun and enjoy the Hmong New Year.* ❞

–Mai See Xiong

❝ *I decided not to go because I know nobody would take me. I'll spend my free time working on my homework and read until the New Year is over.* ❞

–Choua Vang

❝ *I think it will be a little boring because there is hardly anything fun for me to do . . . it will have the usual people walking around looking for someone, kids making airplanes, ball tossing, people playing musical instruments, dancing and a lot of Hmong lullabies. I think that it's a good thing that we still celebrate in Laos and Thailand. . . .I feel that the New Year is going to change a lot considering that we live in America.* ❞

–Betty Chang

73

■ *Dave Moore describes a favorite Hmong pasttime with the help of Xay Thao, Yu Pheng Vu and Yee Chang.*

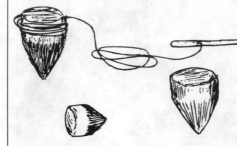

Top wars

Every boy in Laos or in the Thailand refugee camps has a top. In America most do not. And though the older boys here remember playing with tops in Thailand and Laos, the younger ones have generally had no such experience. Thus the older boys in Scout Troop 100 have revived the art of top making, and have taught the craft and game that goes with it to younger scouts.

On weekend camp-outs, the boy scouts of Troop 100 have spent whole days just making and playing with tops. Like any good game, the top game is simple and fun. There are two teams: attackers and defenders. The defenders spin their tops in a defined circle area about ten feet in diameter while the attackers stand behind a straight line drawn about ten feet away. One by one, the attackers try to hit the defenders' tops so that they stop spinning or send it bouncing several yards away. They launch their own tops with an overhand throwing motion. Hitting the opponents' top so hard that it splits in two is considered a major triumph and evokes howls of appreciation from everyone.

There are no arguments, fights or tears in the game of tops. Strategy is not important, though skill is at a premium. There are no captains, as everyone knows what to do. Because there is no score kept, the game has no winners or losers. A highly skilled player can score a lot of hits, and good smashing ones are appreciated even by those whose tops have been hit. One can tell when a top war is going on nearby from all the yelling and laughing.

In the refugee camps, a top is born when a man decides to cut down a tree. After getting permission to do so from the Thai government, he takes his ax and starts to chop. Kids come running toward the sound from all directions to watch the tree fall over. If they ask, the owner may let them have a branch from which to make a top. Younger children may ask an uncle, older brother or parent to make them one.

The Hmong top is a prized possession, and great care is taken of a good one. The harder and heavier the top, the better. Oak is the preferred wood. Designs can be either painted on or carved into the top for a flashy look when it spins. The string which wraps around the top can be made from nearly anything, including: packaging string, twine or fishline, though ideally it is made from a very thin nylon parachute cord. One end of the string is then tied to a stick which is held in a special way to spin the top.

■ *Members of Hmong Boy Scout Troop 100 engage in a game of top in a downtown Minneapolis parking lot.*

Though the game of tops is played constantly, the height of the playing season usually occurs during the annual new year's celebration. Boys between the ages of eight and fourteen will play, though it has traditionally become the main preoccupation of those aged eleven and up. Day after day and hour upon hour the boys play – as if there were no tomorrow. They ignore the choking dust and stifling heat. Nothing matters but the game of tops.

By the age of fourteen, boys have found better things to do at the new year celebration, like throwing ball with the girls (who do not play tops). Yet many will still do it sometimes for fun and social involvement.

Though the top game is violent, the violence is completely vicarious. It doesn't compare with the violence of Hmong pop guns. which shoot small, hard berries that can raise welts and leave black and blue marks. Pop gun wars are more realistic than top wars. Or a boy may take his sling shot and go hunting all day, shooting anything that moves save people. But there is nothing like the feeling of mastery that comes when one smashes his opponent's top out of the circle, and it goes reeling off sideways to a complete stop while the victor's spins on gracefully.

In reviving the art of top making, the older scouts of Troop 100 have spent hours on porch steps or under trees carving tops for younger scouts. They use huge, homemade Hmong knives, holding the blade just right and carefully carving away from themselves so a slip will not cost them a finger. Their reward comes when they hear yelling and laughter, the snapping of strings and the clicking of wood against wood from Hmong boys engaged in Top Wars. ▼

Illustration by Tong Thao

PART TWO

WAR AND EXODUS

▶ THE CROSSING

▶ ESCAPE

▶ MEMORIES OF WAR

▶ LIFE IN LIMBO

The crossing

■ *Dave Moore, Scoutmaster of Hmong Boy Scout Troop 100 and former social studies teacher at Edison High School in Minneapolis.*

Just as they reached camp, it started to rain. There were a few large drops at first, but suddenly it was a pelting thunder storm. The three Scouts dove into their tent, glad to get out if it. But as the rain abated, Pao Choua took some tinder and sticks that he had kept dry, crawled out and built a fire. He added a few more sticks and pretty soon he had a nice blaze. Then he set about preparing dinner for his patrol. The rain continued, just a drizzle now, but no one else stirred out of their tents. The rice bubbled in the pot, the meat and vegetables sizzled in the pan, and Pao Choua thought, "It doesn't get any better than this." He was soaking wet by now but he didn't think about that. He was thinking how hungry he was and how he would soon be sitting around eating rice and chicken with his new American friends.

It had not always been so easy for Pao Choua to get himself something to eat. Before he had ben a Boy Scout in America, he had been a soldier on the other side of the world. His M-16 rifle was almost as tall as he was, and in order to shoot it he had had to rest it on a rock or a fallen tree. That made it almost impossible to use the gun, but as the only surviving male in his family, he had no choice: he was obliged to do it. Things had not gone well at all. A few old rifles were no match against tanks and bombs and gas, and soon he and his fellow soldiers, an army of old men and boys, were running pell-mell through the forest. They ran for many days and nights, moving only when they felt safe, los-

■ *Pathet Lao soldier surprises a Hmong man trying to escape to Thailand. (Pa ndau photo courtesy of the Science Museum of Minnesota)*

ing each other in the darkness, following narrow forest trails and animal tracks or just hacking their way through the jungle, their numbers always diminishing.

Then after many days Pao Choua and two friends, exhausted and hungry, crouched in bushes at the edge of a great river. If they could manage to cross it, they knew they would be free. Pao Choua could swim a little bit, but Xay and Kou not at all. Xay had been limping for the last two days, his big toe swollen and purple. Kou carried the rice, but it had dwindled away to almost nothing. Pao Choua had the only gun and two bullets. From their hide-out, they looked out across the river. They had spoken little for days, and now they spoke not at all. Far on the other side, perhaps a mile away, they could see trucks moving along a road. Down river on their left, the top of a pagoda poked out of trees.

Between them and the river ran a foot-path. The boys watched the path more than they looked across the river. They were small, wiry, bright-eyed mountain boys, hardened from lives spent high above clouds. Neither of them was more than eleven years old.

Pao Choua broke the silence. "I cross tonight. If I make it, I get a boat and come back. Maybe tonight. Maybe tomorrow night."

"What if you don't make it, Pao?" asked Xay. What do we do?"

Pao Choua didn't answer right away. But finally he said, "Don't worry. Don't be scared. You guys are my brothers. I make it. I promise."

Xay and Koua were not Pao Choua's brothers. They were not even members of his clan. They were White Hmongs from a village on the other side of the ridge from his own. He had only know them for a few weeks. But the chances of war had thrown them together and joined them in bonds thicker than

any blood.

From their hideout, the boys watched the sun go slowly down. It sank toward the horizon, turned bright red and dissolved in the pervasive dust of Asia. As soon as it was completely dark, Pao Choua said, "Well, good-bye, brothers. If I don't come back, always remember me. Don't be scared."

The three boys shook hands and then Pao Choua stepped out of the bushes, crossed the path in a crouch and silently, carefully, waded into the river. It was warm and the current was strong. The bottom was soft and sandy, but soon the water was up to his chest and then his neck. He extended his arms, kicked his feet and slowly began to swim. The current carried him along.

Pao Choua did not know how long he was in the river but at last, exhausted, choking and spitting up water, he crawled up onto a sandy bank. He sat and faced the river. It flowed away toward his right side.

That meant he had crossed. He lay down and fell asleep.

Pao Choua spent the next day looking for a boat. The Thai people were curious but not unfriendly. Why do you want a boat?" they asked. "This is Thailand. You're free."

But Pao replied, "I'm a soldier. There are three of us. I have to go back." By nightfall, he had a small, narrow fishing canoe. But the Lao shore was so dark and even that he wasn't sure where his friends were. He paddled noiselessly as he approached the bushes. The path was there, but where were his friends? Was he really at the right place, or were they miles away? He coasted the silent banks, but they did not give up their secret. Squinting into blackness, he scanned the shore. He paddled for a mile and then two: nothing. He whispered, "Xay, Kou," and then he spoke out their names against the darkness, but there was only silence.

■ *Many crossing the river were surprised and shotto death by Pathet Lao guards who patrolled the shoreline. (Pa ndau photo courtesy of the Science Museum of Minnesota)*

■ *Once in Thailand, a Hmong family begs for asylum. (Pa ndau photo courtesy of the Science Museum of Minnesota)*

The night was ebbing away. Somewhere down river a rooster crowed and then another. It would be getting light soon. Pao Choua stood up in the boat. He formed a trumpet with his hands and called out "Xay, Kou! It's me, Pao Choua. I came back. Where are you?"

There was a disturbance in the bushes directly in front of him and two small shapes were darting across the path toward him. Pao Choua didn't see the soldiers on the path or hear their guns, but his canoe was blasted apart from under him and he dove for the bottom. He swam long and long under the water when, with lungs bursting he camp up for air, the current had already swept him far down river and away. He could barely hear the confused, angry voices. He saw flashlight beams playing on the water behind him, but they never came close to him.

It was a long swim back to the Thai shore.

The rain had stopped, clouds were breaking up and a patch of blue sky was already getting larger. Pao Choua called out, "Jack, Bobby. Supper is ready, come on. Eat rice!"

The tent erupted and two scouts tumbled out.

Pao Choua was dishing up three huge platefuls of rice and chicken from the two pots.

"Were you out here making dinner all this time? We could have helped," Said Bobby.

Pao Choua grinned. "It's O.K. No problem. I like to cook."

"Is there anything you can't do, Pao?" asked Jack.

Pao was still grinning, "Yeah, lots of things."

He thought of two other friends somewhere on the other side of the world and his face saddened. Where were they now? Were they hungry? Were they even alive? He shook his head. "Lots of things," he said. He sat down on the ground and started eating his rice. ▼

Escape

Betty Chang

■ *Betty is a seventh grade student at Folwell Jr. High School in Minneapolis. She is the second oldest daughter of Sia Chang and Mai Hang. (Photo by Dan Hess)*

An interview with Mai Hang

I liked living in Laos when there was no war. We had freedom to do what we wanted. When you went somewhere you didn't have to worry about being scared because there were no bad people. Each family farmed for themselves and spent their days in the fields in peace and quiet. Every family owned a house, farmland, and animals. Sometimes we sold our animals and harvest in exchange for money. Then we traded money in for fabric to make clothes. We also bought other things such as cooking utensils.

Not long after our peaceful and good life, the war began. We heard that the war was started as a result of a dispute between two Lao brothers who both wanted control over Laos. One was a Communist who sided with the North Vietnamese. Around 1960, most of the Hmong men became soldiers, fighting Communist forces who were trying to take over the country.

We heard bombs exploding far away in the distance. We heard the firing of guns from all over the northern parts of Laos. At this time, many people had to move

81

■ *Life in Laos prior to the Vietnam War is pictured here: weeding rice field and grinding corn. (Pa ndau photo courtesy of the Science Museum of Minnesota)*

their villages to avoid the war. People could not work in the farms anymore. Some of them had already became refugees. Others followed their sons or husbands who became soldiers so they can get free food.

Hundreds and thousands of Hmong men and boys were killed in the war.

After fifteen years of constant fighting with the Communist Lao and North Vietnamese, Laos was finally taken over by the invaders. Vang Pao, the first Hmong to be ranked General, was determined to fight the Communists to the end, but in 1975 when the country was overrun, he left with other Lao leaders to Thailand.

At the time when we heard the General had left the country, we were still busy planting rice and had not worry about leaving our country. Other people were following the General. Those who could not get on airplanes took buses, cars, and taxis. Most began their long trek by walking westward to Thailand. One week after the flood of people leaving Laos, Lee Tech, one of the Hmong leaders ordered Communist soldiers to stop the mass of people and kill them all. Some were already half way to Thailand. The killing was mostly around Ban Hin Herb, an area half way between the major Hmong concentration and the Thai border.

Frightened for their lives, people took to the jungle to hide. For most, survival means finding a way to reach Thailand and freedom. Some returned to their villages with little or nothing left. Maybe about half the people who went the Thailand route actually made it. Those who encountered soldiers were killed. Survivors went back to their villages only to find their houses burnt and ruined.

The Communists had taken over. My family was very sad because some of our relatives had left. We could not leave with to be with them because Communist soldiers were everywhere in our village. I remember when they first appeared in our village. They were very polite to us. But I knew that they were only pretending to be nice. They wanted the village leaders and young men, some of them had never worn a soldier uniform, to learn the Communist rules. We knew they would take them away to teach and train them, then kill them. Everyone would get more frighten when someone did not come home from these training sessions. We were scared of the Communists, and did not trust them.

The young men and former CIA soldiers left their villages for the jungle because they knew it was the only safe place. The only chance family members have to see and be with them was when they went farming on the hills near the jungle. Family members would bring them food and tell them what was happening in the village.

The communist soldiers saw that all the young men were nowhere to be seen. Only the elderly people, women, and children were left in the village. They got very angry at everyone. They were especially furious at parents and wives. They took many of the fathers to their bunkers to punish and keep as prisoners. They demanded to know where the young men were. Most fathers and wives didn't tell them. And they killed a couple of the fathers of the young men.

When the news reached the young men that some of their parents were killed, they took out their guns, which had been hidden in the jungle before the Communists came. Many Communist forts and bunkers were attacked by our men, killing a good number of Communist soldiers. After they had been attacked, they left the areas surrounding the villages. They were busy building bigger forts elsewhere. I guess they were afraid of our young CIA soldiers.

Not too long after, they appeared again, this time with an army of tanks, big guns, and planes. They

started bombing our homes, valleys, and our mountains. We could hear and see the bombs exploding all around the outskirts of our village. We could not live in the village anymore. It was decided that everyone must go to the jungle to hide. But we must stay close enough to our farm so that it would be easier to get food. We lived like this for many months.

The Communists continued bombing our villages. They wanted to scare us and ultimately make us surrender. But no one would leave the jungle. One afternoon, just after lunch we heard bombs exploding far away. Then they came closer and closer. Suddenly we were surrounded by explosions of fire. It did not stop for many hours. We tried to cover ourselves and stayed low to the ground. Some people near us were killed. My father told us to go south and then west towards Thailand. We did not know where we were because the

■ *Vietnamese and Pathet soldiers fire at fleeing Hmong villagers. (Pa ndau photo courtesy of the Science Museum of Minnesota)*

83

■ *Escaping Hmong could be fired upon along the trail by Pathet Lao and Vietnamese soldiers. (Pa ndau photo courtesy of the Science Museum of Minnesota)*

jungle was too thick and dark.

We decided we would not stay and fight anymore. Even if no one knew the way there, we were determined to reach Thailand because we could no longer stand the day to day life in the jungle. Many of our cousins and other Hmong people got together for a meeting. Each family would carry enough rice, cooking pots, and some clothes for the journey. We started out heading south, with the Communists gaining behind us. We walked up and down hills, across valleys and up again to the mountains where there is no path. We walked all afternoon and all night. We had crossed over a big chain of mountains to the other side, and felt safer.

We soon came upon some Hmong people who had escaped from their villages and were on the same path towards Thailand. We saw that many among those were wounded, and others crying end-

lessly. Some of the people wanted to go eastward, because there was a part of the country that had not been attacked and overrun by the Communists yet. The rest of the people wanted to go to Thailand.

No one had a map. So no one knew the way there. We did not know how far and how many days it would take to get there. No one knew if it would even going to be safe. In spite of all this uncertainty, we still wanted to go. It was the only better choice. So, all we knew was to keep going west and we would reach Thailand

The leaders divided us into smaller groups, by clan and relatives. The group that both my husband's family and my family belong to had about forty-five people. At the time, we were running out of food and had barely enough left. We decided it was time to leave when night came. This way, no one will see us or find the traces that we left behind.

It was about seven in the evening when we started out. At four in the morning, we passed by a communist village. We went around it so they notice us, but their dogs knew and they barked at us all night long. When morning came, we were making our way through the villagers' rice fields. We wanted to run and be cleared off the open field before there was light, but could not because there were too many of us together. Some communist villagers coming to work the fields saw us but did not stop us.

We continued walking all day until we could not go on anymore. By then, we had only one bottle of water left. We were very thirsty and hungry. It would be dark soon, so we decided to make camp on top of a hill. There was a river at the bottom of the hill and some of the men went to get some water to make food. We all went to sleep.

The communist villagers who saw earlier must have told the men in the village that we had passed by. At about three in the morning, I heard some noise coming from the jungle. At first, I thought it sounded like twigs or sticks breaking. I sat up and looked around, but saw nothing. I was too scared to go back to sleep, so I laid there quietly and listened. An hour had passed. Then I saw something like a candle in the forest. After a while I heard something like a bird crying. But, I suspect it must be the Pathet Lao soldiers signaling to each other. When the whistling stopped, another would start. The sound was unusual. They made it sound like birds crying. But when birds cry, they cry together, not one at a time. I got really scared so I woke up my brother. He did not hear anything and went back to sleep.

The morning came and we were already starting to cook breakfast when gunfire burst out from the trees. They took us by surprise, wounded many and some killed on the spot. It was chaos, everyone was running in every direction. An hour later we all found each other, the people in my family. Most of

our belongings were missing. Other people returned to the site of the ambush and found their knives.

The communists that shot us were not soldiers, only villagers. They had taken our things and shown them to our cousins who surrendered and now lived the communists.

We had nothing left. When we got hungry, we ate the inside parts of banana trees, bamboo, and leaves from plants and trees. On our trek, we saw people who had died from stepping on mines. We got very scared.

We still did not know exactly where we were or which way to. We knew only to follow the sun when it goes down. Every few days, someone would climb a tall tree on a mountain to see if we were still going the right way. We came across a river called Nam Ngia. It was our first test to see how we can get across a river. There, we set camp and practiced

■ *Survival in the wilderness was difficult for Hmong who were on the run from Pathet Lao and Vietnamese soldiers. (Pa ndau photo courtesy of the Science Museum of Minnesota)*

■ *The Mekong River crossing was another obstacle to be dealt with.*
(Pa ndau photo courtesy of the Science Museum of Minnesota)

how to build and use a raft. The men cut each person six small pieces of bamboo, each a yard long and lashed it together with vines. We practiced using the rafts we made in the river for two days. We knew we would eventually use these skills in the big Mekong River.

But we still did not know how far away the Mekong was, and if we ever get there. We traveled ten more days, over a big mountain range to the other side. By then, we knew that the Thai border was not too far off. There, we cut enough bamboo every person. At noon the next day, we had climbed a tall mountain and to rest at a rocky plateau with no trees. We looked out west and saw the Mekong River in the far horizon, like a winding yellow road. Below the rocky mountain was a flat and endless valley stretching towards Thailand.

We broke camp there for the night. We hid our leftover rice and our other belongings in a nearby cave in case we run into trouble and needed to come back. We heard that many people had trouble when they came to the Mekong. And if they could not cross it, they could make the trip back to the cave and get food and supplies that were left behind.

We divided our silver savings among family members to carry since no one was sure what would happen on the way to the Mekong. So, we waited until sunset, until the people in their fields went home for the day. We started descending down the mountain cliffs and across the flatlands towards the river. We reached the shore of the Mekong at eleven that evening. Luckily, there weren't Communist soldiers around. We have heard that many were killed at the river, but kept our hopes high. Everyone knew what to do; we quickly tied our rafts together, all in less than a few minutes. Each family was then tied together with a long rope. The better swimmers would lead. Parents with small children or babies put them on their backs.

After about five hours of floating with the current of the water, our our feet finally touched the sand. We knew we had reached Thailand. We didn't have anything with us except for the money that our parents had given us to carry. Some families had drifted away during the crossing, and we didn't know if they had made it. Only one family made it with us. Everyone was cold, especially the younger children who seemed so cold we thought they would die. So, we started a fire and got warmed.

We had just caught our breath when two men approached. They told us not to be afraid anymore because we had reached Thailand. They would help us, they said. They also said that we have valuables, and they would take us to a refugee camp because there are a lot of bad people around the border and they might rob us. We told them we didn't bring anything with us. They didn't believe us, and searched everyone. When they discovered we had money, the demanded we give it to them. They would let us go free, they said. If we refuse, they would beat us. Finally, I gave some to them without any trouble because I was afraid that they would not let us live.

They treated us like prisoners, and we all thought we were still in Laos and have not made it to Thailand. When they got the money, they said they would bring us some food, clothing, and someone to get us to the camp, but they never came back. We got very scared because of the way they treated us, and everyone started crying. We waited a while and four Thai soldiers came. They were Thai Border Securities and they would help. We need not be afraid anymore. They put us in the back of their army truck and took us to their station. There, we met part of the group who crossed the river with us, and we knew hat the Thai soldiers had helped them too.

We had really made it to Thailand. And for that, we were happy about. They gave us clothing and food, then took us to the immigration office. We stayed at the office for two days, then they moved us to Non Khai Refugee Camp. When we got there, we saw a lot of people we knew, including my uncle and his family. They were one of the first people to come to Thailand. My older brother and his family were there too. I was so happy to see them. Everyone chipped in to help us buy bamboo and hay to build a little hut by their house. We each had only one pair of clothes, so they donated us a few extra to change with. ▼

An interview with Blong Yang

By Paul Yang

Blong Yang was born in Sam Thong on April 4, 1970. The eldest son and the second child of Ntsuab Txos Yaj, a head member in the village.

Everyday life in the village included chores in which everyone was involved. Blong had to get up early to find firewood and prepare breakfast. After breakfast, there were cattle and crops that had to be tended. Crops were a major part of everyone's life. Blong's family crop consisted of corn, beans, cabbage, herbs, sugarcane, lettuce, onions, and tomatoes. If family members worked hard tending their crops, there would be plenty to eat and sell at harvest time. If members were lazy, the family would starve

Paul Yang

■ *Paul is the son of Phia Yang and a Patrol Leader in Boy Scout Troop 100.*

■ *Life before war was year-round hard work growing rice and corn. Above, a farmer picks the first corn (pob kws tshab). (Pa ndau photo courtesy of the Science Museum of Minnesota)*

while watching others' plentiful harvests.

Just as Blong turned six, war broke out in the countryside. Frightened by the thought of death, Blong's father decided it was time to move away.

At the age of seven, Blong started school, where he learned English, Thai, and French. It was English, however, that Blong was most interested in. At the first grade level, these languages were basic building blocks of what was yet to come.

The sounds of war drew closer, and Blong's father gathered his family to flee. From "Teb Chaws Los Tsuas" to Keo Sa Khay, then on to Muang Hom.

Crossing the Mekong River was a challenge for some, easy for others. It was challenging for those who couldn't afford a boat ride. Many were forced to drift across in inner tubes, or rafts made by binding together large clusters of bamboo. Still others swam the great river. A group of people would tie themselves together with a long rope and let the best swimmer go first. Swept up in the current, groups would sometimes drift for hours.

Blong had to cross the Mekong River alone. He had promised his parents that he would try to get a better education in America. So Blong left his family behind with tears in his eyes and a strong spirit in his heart. The boat ride across the Mekong River was quick and fast. Feeling safe and free, Blong arrived in Thailand.

Life in the refugee camps of Thailand was not easy. The Hmong felt unwanted. Houses were built of wood, some raised on stilts, others on the ground with dirt floors. Management of the Thai refugee camps was very disciplined. There were strict rules. The camps were surrounded by barbed wire fences, and anyone caught trying to leave the premises would be penalized and fined. There was also the possibility of being taken to jail, beaten, tortured, and even put to death.

Despite severe penalties, life in the refugee camps could also be rewarding. For all the restrictions, residents still had some freedom to associate with family, relatives and friends; Yet it was hard on many who came alone.

Arriving in America was a new experience. There were new things and many people of different races. America was an exciting and scary place, with new treasures and dangers.

Living in America for four and a half months, Blong is attending night school at Central Sr. High to try and complete a General Equivalence Degree. He hopes to eventually go on to college and a better life in America than "Teb Chaws Los Tsuas." ▼

■ *Va Vang is pictured at left with his father Chue Kou Vang (photo by Dan Hess). His family is pictured below in Thailand along the banks of the Mekong River. (Family photo)*

An interview with Chue Kou Vang

I was born in March, 1936. My parents were Nhia Vang and Mai Yang.

I became a soldier for the French on April 8, 1952 at the age of 14. In 1955-56, I was stationed at Kan Kai village for 8 months. I became an officer there. When I got back from Kan Kai, I helped my family in the fields, planting rice and corn. I went to war in 1960, but lost to the army of Kong Le. They returned back to Mongonlee, a Hmong village, to set up a fortified camp. From 1962-67, I advanced through 5 ranks. In 1975 we lost our areas to the Communists. I was captured by the Communist soldiers in November, 1975, but escaped. I left Laos in January 1976 and went to Thailand.

On June 9, 1977, I went back to Laos as a soldier for the resistance. While I was back, I got married. On July 17, 1977 my oldest daughter Pa was born. Two years passed and my family decided to go to Thailand. At just about that time, on May 6, 1979, my son Va was born.

Two months later, we crossed the Mekong River to Thailand. My family was afraid that my son Va might drown in the river, so he was carried piggy back by my sister See. Crossing the river was the hardest part, but we made it. We came to the United States in 1980. Here in America, I work with my brother at his auto shop. ▼

Memories of War

■ *Clockwise from left: You Mai Chang in 1969 at Long Cheng, the flag of Laos prior to 1975, Tong Noi village in the mountains of Xiengkhouang province. (Chang family photos)*

■ *Resistance forces in mid 80s near Thailand/Laos border. (Courtesy of Bruce Xiang)*

■ *At left is Chia Ye Xiong in 1974 (courtesy of Chia Ye Xiong). Above, Yang Dang, Boua Yee and Pang Lee Chang in 1966 near Mt. Phu Bia. (Courtesy of Yang Dang Chang)*

91

■ *Clockwise from above left: Long Cheng in 1975, the U.S. "secret" air strip (photo by Sia Chang), Cher Pao Thao, a Hmong soldier in the CIA secret army, and a view of the Mekong looking across from Thailand toward Laos (photo by Dave Moore).*

■ *Clockwise from above: drawing by Tong Thao of a family being strafed by Pathet Lao and Vietnamese gunfire while attempting to swim to freedom across the Mekong River, Chong Ze Moua in 1973 as a soldier in Long Cheng (courtesy of Blia Moua and Chong Phia Yang), and two brothers of Shu Yang (courtesy of Kia Xiong).*

13 A life in limbo

■ *Refugee camp identification picture of Cher Pao Thao's family. HYCAP member Tong Thao is center front. (Courtesy of Thao family)*

On the other side of the world, nestled into a little glen in the hills of northern Thailand, is a place that was once unlike any other place. Camp Ban Vinai, deserted now, was once a city of 40,000 people crammed into five square kilometers. All the residents of the city were Hmong refugees from Laos. Some of them lived there for a few weeks before moving on to countries of final refuge. Many others lived there for ten years or more. they remembered building the camp in the mid-seventies. Over half the residents were minors, more than a third small children. For a whole Hmong generation, camp life was the only home they knew. They never saw rice growing on an upland hillside. They never rode on the back of a huge, patient water buffalo. They were never shaken gently awake in the early hours and told, "We're going hunting." They never stood on a mountain top amid opium poppies, looking out over a wilderness of silent peaks lost in morning mist. They never smelled the pungent, acrid smoke that hung over the whole countryside as the Hmong burned off the hills in their annual preparation for a new planting.

What did they experience, these children of a lost generation? What did they all experience, the residents of the largest city of Hmong people ever assembled in one place? To find out, let's turn back the clock and drop in on this camp as it was in the late seventies:

One day in Ban Vinai is like all the others. By 4:00 a.m. the whole camp is awake. Cook fires are stirred up and the day's rice is being prepared. By mid-morning, the camp throbs with life. Little children are everywhere, many of them bare naked in the steamy heat generated by the sun and the crowded humanity. There are so many games to play: pitching games, running games, games with home-made tops. There are things to watch, and whenever anything happens, there is a crowd of kids hanging around to gawk and be in the way. The camp soccer field fills up with older boys and young men playing several simultaneous games of soccer. There are more than the regulation number of players on each team, but the play is fast and furious nonetheless, and the athletes perform with matchless grace and ability. Pretty girls in bright-colored parasols stroll around the camp in groups of two or three. Women gather in front of their compounds and take up their beautiful embroidery and their endless talk.

But there is work to be done. The rice distribution must be claimed and carried home. Water must be lugged from the water stations. Language classes get started. The Thai soldiers who guard the camp may have some work for the residents, and that has to be attended to before all else. Along the camp's main street and dotted all over it, little shops run by residents sell all kinds of things. You can buy anything in Ban Vinai. Just put in your order.

Toward afternoon, as the hot Asian sun climbs across the meridian, the pace of life slows, just perceptibly. The children don't know it's hot and keep on playing. But others retire to the shade of their tiny, crowded dwellings, remove sandals and sit on comfortable little bamboo porches where there may be some air stirring. The women keep on with their fancy needlework. The men sit and talk. There is seldom any news to talk about, but the damp lives on rumors. There is talk of the resistance still going on in Laos; of the possibility of the Thai and Lao governments patching up a deal which would leave the Hmong out in the cold, since they are at the moment a convenient buffer for the Thais. There is talk of America. For these last refugees of the Vietnam War, there is nothing left but hope, and even that is slowly dying in Ban Vinai as the residents adjust, willy-nilly, to camp life.

Then at last the sun turns red in the suffocating haze, there is a little relief, and night comes on. The day in camp is over. Tomorrow will be the same.

■ *Yee Chang is pictured as a resident of Ban Vinai Refugee Camp in Northern Thailand from 1979-80.*

An interview with Yee Chang

Yee chang was a resident of the Ban Vinai Refugee Camp in northern Thailand. His family swam the Mekong river to escape the war in Laos. The following interview was conducted by Dave Moore.

Housing

We lived in the new section of the camp where the houses are made out of bamboo and leaves, grass, and the ground is just dirt. These houses are long houses. They divide the houses into different rooms. Each family gets a room. The room is just one room and we just kind of made dividers for sleeping and for cooking. It's pretty small. It wasn't strange but it was just crowded, because we weren't used to living with neighbors on both sides of the wall. You could hear everything. People walking in and out of each other's living space, because that's how you get from one place to another. So you just walk right through people's living room.

Daily Routine

Usually I wake up pretty early, I think six or seven. Six o'clock everybody's up. Sometimes four o'clock for people who go out to the market.

I just play around. Hang out. My mom sells stuff, sells vegetables. So I just go and hang around the market. Just play all day. Just roam around. It's a pretty big place, so there's always new things to see. Just look for stuff.

There wasn't much room for tops, so we played with rubber bands. We got them from the market, where they use a lot of rubber bands. So kids pick them up and play around. Trade rubber bands. Have little contests where you tie rubber bands together and try to hit it and break it apart and however many you break apart you get. So we have different teams and play for rubber bands.

We play soccer with anything that's around. Such as a doll's head or anything. No ball.

There were a lot of us, maybe a dozen or so. Hanging out. A sling shot was another good thing. We'd shoot birds and things like that. Shoot anything, shoot lizards. You've got this dead bird and you just build a fire and cook it. And eat it.

Go fishing. There was a man-made lake. You just build a fire and cook and eat. That's your whole day. That's the adventure of the day.

I get home when it gets dark. I

have to come home. There's not much to do because it's dark. Just eat dinner and go to bed.

Meals

Dinner is usually rice and something. Vegetables. I don't think I was hungry, but you didn't always have meat. Just once in a while, or if you could afford to buy it. But we didn't buy because they distribute meat once every two weeks. We'd have meat a couple of times. The pork was O.K., but the fish was bad. The fish couldn't be eaten. It's really salty and not very good. I don't know, you just have to try it.

School

I didn't go to school. There were schools but I never went to school. I knew other kids who went to school.

Work

I helped my brother a couple of times. He carried water for a Thai family who lived right by the camp gate. Each time, he carried about

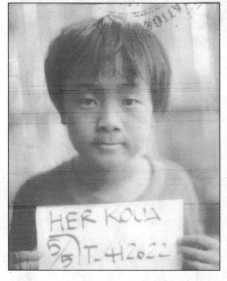

■ *Above, the main market street in Ban Vinai Refugee Camp (photo by Dave Moore). At left is a camp I.D. picture of Koua Her.*

two bucketful. I don't know how he found the job, but he had been working for a while. The Thai family gave him a couple of Baht. I helped a few of times. I spent the few Bahts I earned on candy. Candy was a big thing. If your mom gave you a Baht or two you would save and buy candy, such as gum and wrapped candy, like lollypops.

Sickness, Death, Violence

There was a lot of sickness. A lot

97

■ *A whole generation of children was born in the camp since it opened in 1976. (Photo by Dave Moore)*

The drums played all the time. People come and go. People hang around to talk, play cards, or just watch the ceremonies.

There was a cemetery in the camp, a Hmong cemetery. There were no markings on the grave. But you can tell there were different types of graves, depending on which family or clan and what their tradition is. Not all Hmong have the very same tradition. Some graves have rocks stacked on top to form a hill. Others just pile dirt over the top. Some are just flat and you can't see them. My family's tradition is to cover it with dirt only.

The cemetery was spooky because people were buried there all the time. Sometimes I got really scared just walking near the place. People don't stay out too late. When it gets dark, the place looks different, and you don't want to be alone.

A lot of bad things happen in the camp. The ones I heard about were robbery, beating, and murder. When there are so many people together, a lot of things can happen. People sneak in and out of the camp. I guess there was all kinds of illegal things going on. For one thing, the camp is not a permanent place to live. And people would do anything just to get by, sometimes they get into trouble with the Thai camp guards.

The Thai guards were in charge. People deferred to them. They control everything, and get mad whenever they want. They order people

of death, too. I don't know what kind of sickness there were. I've never been to the hospital in Ban Vinai so I don't know what it's like in there. People were afraid of being sick.

But you always knew when there was death. Almost every day there was death somewhere in the camp. And the drums would play. When somebody died, a traditional Hmong funeral was held and usually attracted everyone's attention. You can hear the drums from anywhere in the camp. During a Hmong funeral, many things go on. People play the drums and the kheng, and they chant songs for the dead. Different families are invited to come and pay respect by killing animals for the dead. A funeral was usually big, and there was food there. Many people go attend. Funerals were kind of public. They have it right in front of the house. So anyone can go. It usually last a couple of days -- two, three days.

around and people do what they say because they have the guns. If someone got in trouble with the guards, they have to have money to pay them, or be taken away

The place really is a prison. You can't go out, unless you want to get shot. I've heard of people who were beaten really bad. They go out to collect firewood or something, get caught , and beaten to death.

The Camp as Metaphor

Even in America people still have the sense that they are still in a camp. The old folks have it the most. In this country, because of the language barrier, because of the different culture, they feel they are locked in and have no way out. They can't do what they want.

Maybe for some of younger generation, too, who grew up here. They don't know what their parents experienced in Laos and Thailand. They don't see how importance it is to be in this country. There are so many opportunities here. Some are neither serious with school nor with their own culture because they don't recognize the pain and struggle our parents went through.

In America, I have to learn how to get out of the camp psychology. To do that, it seems you have to blend in and know what's going on. At the same time that you learn about America, you should also appreciate your culture. In this way, I think you can break away from feeling trapped in some kind of camp. We should learn and understand our parents and the real camp that they suffered through

and survived. I have realized that we have it better here because of the struggles of our parents. I a m thankful that I am no longer physically trapped inside barb wires and trenches. ▼

Interview with Mai Hang

This is the continuation of an interview conducted by Betty Chang. In it, Mai Hang tells of camp life in preparation for immigration to the United States.

Everyone must stay inside the camp compound. A United Nations program was there to distribute free food but it was never enough. There was a shortage of food, water, and clothing. Our life had been so hard in Laos and it was the same in Thailand.

We were free and safe in Thailand, yet we still didn't know what the future had in store for us. After three months, my relatives said they had already signed some papers to come to America. We moved into their house when they left for the U.S.

Refugee Camp Non Khai was divided into two sections, one for Laotian refugees, which is two thirds of the camp, and the other for Hmong. Most of the meat and food were passed through the Laotian camp before they were delivered to the Hmong. In May 1979, many Hmong were poisoned by eating the food they distributed. The Camp clinic was so full of sick people that some had to be sleep outside. The incident lasted two

■ *After interviews at camp and a long wait, some families were on their way to a new life in another culture.*
(Pa ndau photo courtesy of the Science Museum of Minnesota)

days; most were treated, released and were fine. They hadn't delivered the food to my group yet, so I wasn't poisoned.

We lived there for another month when we heard that we were going to have to move to Ban Vinai, a camp for just Hmongs. My first child, Alee was born in Nong Khai on June 18. In August, many buses came and picked us up for Ban Vinai. The bus ride was long; it took almost a whole day to get there. When we arrived, United Nations programs had already built long bamboo buildings for us to live in. It was divided into small sections, and there was hardly any space to cook, eat and sleep.

Thai leaders granted permission for Hmongs to go out of the camp to get building materials. After the construction, no one was allowed outside the camp. If anyone disobeyed, Thai securities would torture them.

There was not enough water. So, we dug up a well. We used it cooking even though it smelled bad and was yellow. In the camp, there was a lot of sickness and death, and I

wanted to get away.

In a short time, my husband was chosen as a food distributor for a section of the camp. There are eight sections, each section is divided quarters, which are then divided into houses, and then rooms or sections of the house.

Two months later, the Americans came to Ban Vinai to interview the families who had been working for the CIA in Laos and want to resettle in America. We decided to apply for an interview and if we passed the interview and paper work, we could go to America.

On December 18, 1979 they announced that my family could leave for Bangkok on the 21st. Our relatives got together for the last time. We talked and cried a lot because only my husband, my daughter and I were going to leave. We were leaving my in-laws and my family behind. At that time, there was no way to know what things would be like on the other side of the world. We had no way of knowing what would happen to those who stayed either. It was a hard situation. We didn't know if we would ever see each other again.

We packed whatever we owned and got ready. On the morning of December 21st we went to the big soccer field in the middle of the Camp. Ten buses were waiting to pick us up. The loudspeakers families to board the buses. As soon as we stepped on the bus, my heart broke and I thought that things will change forever since I will be on the other side of the world, in America. I remember my family reaching up their hands to the windows of the bus, crying and wishing us good luck, and saying they hope we would see each other again. Everyone was crying so hard because parting just hurt so much.

We were on our way to Bangkok, then the U.S.A. My husband and I cried all the way to Bangkok. We arrived at midnight. The camp was only for people who were on their way to the U.S. or another country. There were two big buildings for people to stay in, and the rest had to live in tents. We had to sleep on the ground under the tents for five days. They cooked food for us but we were very hungry still. On the 26th they posted a list of the people board a plane the next day, but we didn't see our names. We were patient and went back to our place under the tent to sleep. In the middle of the night, at two o'clock, and still sleeping, they called our identification numbers (T Numbers). We were surprised to hear our names because we weren't on the list. We got ready as fast as we could and ran to the gate in time to catch the bus to the airport.

We changed planes so many times, once in Taipei, then Seoul, where it was snowing and very cold because we were in our regular clothes from Thailand. It was the first time we saw snow. We were on the plane for only a little while when it was light again and we didn't understand it. Finally, we landed in Honolulu International Airport in Hawaii. There, we were greeted by my husband's relatives. It had been a long journey and finally we were in America.

They took us to their apartment building, which had sixteen floors, and they lived on the eighth. They prepared all kinds of food for us but we couldn't eat. We were so exhausted. We slept for a week recovering from the trip.

My husband had cousins and relatives so he was happy, but none of mine lived in Honolulu so I was sad. My husband, my daughter and I live with one of my husband's uncles named Wang Mang Chang. They worked all day and in the evening, we get to eat with them. During the time when they were at work, we didn't know how to turn on the stove and use the electric rice cooker. So everyday we were hungry. We didn't know how to use the phone so we couldn't call anyone to talk to. We only looked out the window.

We applied for AFDC and they gave us Food Stamps to buy food. Later, we found a one bedroom apartment. At that time, we only had three plates, three spoons, one pot and one electric rice cooker from my husband's cousin Nchaiv Fwj. We still have the same rice cooker now, after all these years. We had one full size mattress, but no sheets. No table but two chairs. Though we were in America, we were very lonely and we missed our family who were still in Thailand.

One and a half months later, my

■ *Bound for Ameica, Hmongs are escorted to their planes. (Pa ndau photo courtesy of the Science Museum of Minnesota)*

husband's parents, brothers, and sisters joined us from Thailand. I cry a lot because I was sad. But I was happy that we had escaped from the war and now we can finally live a good life.

In Hawaii we had a lot of freedom. We would go to the park and stay there till dark without being harmed. Hawaii was a lot like Laos. It had the same tropical weather. The trees and grass were always green and beautiful. The same kind of plants, fruits, even sugar canes grows there. Some of the things that was different were the elevators, stoves, beds, and the houses.

We didn't want to leave Hawaii, but we had to because our cousins were moving. On march 1st 1981, my second daughter, Betty was born. We had to move to the mainland because there were more Hmongs there. We decided to come to Minnesota where many of our relatives have already settled. We didn't have enough money for the plane tickets , but our relatives in Minneapolis and St. Paul collected enough money for our the tickets. We missed Hawaii.

It was summer when we arrived in Minneapolis. The trees were green and we liked it a lot. But when fall came, the trees changed and not long after, it started getting colder and then it snowed. We did not like it. We had no idea what to wear for the cold weather. I found out the hard way not to dry clothes outside in the winter; my clothes were frozen hard. It was very strange.

After a year, I got used to the weather changes in mainland America, especially Minnesota. We like it here in the U.S. because there is enough food, clothes, and places for people to live in. The people are healthy and everyone has a chance to go to school; to learn how to read and write English.

But it is very difficult for me and the other grown-ups to learn the English language because back in Laos, we did not have a formal education. In the U.S., it is a first for us to go to school. We learned how to write our names. At first, we didn't know the letters in our names, or how to pronounce them. We just remembered how they looked and how they are arranged.

Now I have four more children, all of whom were born in Minneapolis. Chua, born in 1982, Dao in 1983, Fue in 1984, and Xung in 1987. My husband and I are both working now. We are very happy living in the U.S., and that our children have a chance to get a good education, and have good jobs someday. We can now have a good future. ▼

PART THREE

LIFE IN AMERICA

▶ TURNING POINT
▶ BOY SCOUTS
▶ CAUGHT BETWEEN CULTURES
▶ HOPES FOR THE FUTURE

Turning Point

I was afraid of water. I didn't know how to swim. My only security was a rope that was tied around my waist, connecting me to my oldest brother. We waded out into the quiet river, my whole family — all eight of us. Nobody spoke. We had to be completely quiet, silent, and we understood each other communicating only by touch and/or eye contact. By the light of the moon I could see across the water to a low line of trees and, just above the trees, a thin strip of land. Between me, my family and the far shore stretched the dark Mekong River, the last obstacle to freedom.

We waded out farther into the warm, dark water. It was calm and had a thick, muddy, swamp-like feeling as we parted the waves with our hands to make way. Soon my feet were not touching bottom. I hung onto a plastic air bag and kicked my feet back and forth trying to stay afloat. My father and two older brothers could swim and were in front, pulling the rope that connected

Yee Chang
■ *Youth Coordinator of HYCAP, Yee is a graduate of St. Olaf College.*

■ *Finding food to eat could be difficult while constantly on the run. (Pa ndau photo courtesy of the Science Museum of Minnesota)*

period of drying, we set flame to the dead and dried rain forest. The burning stench rose above the barren hills where rice would be planted.

Spinning wooden tops was a favorite game of mine. My village buddies divided themselves into teams, usually according to relation since there were three clans sharing the village compound. One team set their cone-shaped tops spinning on the ground while the other team tried to knock or break them in mid-spin with theirs own.

At night, we listened to the distant sounds of war, sounds which I thought would never come closer. We could tell the difference between the sound of a missile being launched and the sound it made on impact. We even tried guessing the range of the missiles by counting the time between shot and hit.

During the day, my parents busied themselves in the rice field, and I always went along. My brother was issued an M-16 rifle by the Americans so we could protect ourselves. One night, my uncles came to our house and gathered around the fire pit to talk about my distant cousin who was shot and then mutilated in the river while crossing to Thailand. There was other news about babies who were given opium to quiet them down during the crossing. Babies who were given too much stayed forever quiet. I listened quietly, hoping I wouldn't be given opium.

After the Americans left in 1975, the Hmong who served as Ameri-

each of us at the waist. I could feel the little jerks and the tightening of the rope around my waist with each pull. But I was so numbed by the fear of being spotted, captured, and butchered by the communist Lao guards, that I didn't notice the scorching pain.

Caught in the aftermath of the Vietnam War, my family and I, along with tens of thousands of other Hmong people, were pushed out of Laos by the invading Communist forces. We had been peaceful rice farmers living in small villages and raising pigs and chickens. I remember the village life before the "Red Vietnamese" came. I hunted squirrels and orange songbirds with a crossbow my father crafted. We grew rice on the steep mountain slopes. Before rice was planted, the dense jungle had to be cleared by hand, using axes and long knives. The small underbrush and towering teakwoods were severed to knee-high stumps. After a ca's secret army for the CIA were left to fend for themselves. It was a harsh reality that the Hmong were targeted for extermination. There was no place to hide except in the jungle. My family had been wandering and hiding in the jungle for a month, living off small rations of rice, wild roots, leaves, and small animals, trying to find a way to the river and across to Thailand, and to freedom. We left our village with our closest relatives, but were soon joined by hundreds of others seeking the same path. One old man who was too old and weak to walk was given a day's meal of rice and a small amount of raw opium so he could poison himself.

In every direction we faced a wall of jungle, and the adult men hacked away a rough path with their knives. We avoided roads, small paths and open spaces, fearing ambush and capture. We descended a small hill and passed by a village, deserted except for some homeless dogs and the smell of decay.

My job during the journey was to carry the family rice pot, some plates, and a few spoons in a wicker back-pack made to fit around my shoulder blades, which stuck out like fins on my back.

During our trek, we had to surrender to a Communist-controlled village to keep from starving. They were kind and offered us food, and we were allowed to build our own shelters on the edge of the village. Two other families, who earlier had been with us along the journey, had

escaped the village the week before, and the village leaders had supplied guards to watch the compound more carefully. But, late one night, I was awakened by my father and was told we were going hunting. I was excited and got up frantically, but without a word. Quietly, we slipped out into the darkness behind the thick bushes just 20 feet away from our shelter. The rest of my family had already gathered there, crouched down so that I could only see only the whites of their eyes as they looked up. I held on to my brother's shirt tail and followed his quick footsteps in front of me as we escaped into the night.

We walked all night and rested around noon the following day atop a mountain. The air was thin, the ground sharp with rocks, and vegetation was scarce. I was amazed to see strange trees with small green needles. Looking behind I saw the rugged and scaly mountains of Laos. Looking ahead,

■ Escaping Hmong could be fired upon along the trail by Vietnamese soldiers. (Pa ndau photo courtesy of the Science Museum of Minnesota)

105

■ *The Chang family atop a mountain overlooking the valley of the Mekong River. Photo was taken in 1979, two days before crossing the river to safety in Thailand (Chang family collection).*

I saw the rolling lowlands and the peaceful haze of Thailand. My father pointed to something in the deep valley, apparently hidden by the distance. I was told it was the Mekong River, a shinny strip of yellow dividing two pieces of land. It was so far away that I squinted my eyes to bring it closer. I saw the glitter and imagined how good it would feel to jump in its waters and quench my dying thirst.

The descent into the valley took us two days. We reached the lowland by late afternoon and relaxed our eroded knee and ankle joints. They trembled from the stretched and uneven steps our descent. Swampy rice paddies extended into the distance from the foot of the mountain toward the shoreline of the river. A cement road ran parallel to the river. We waited until night, then dashed across the open

field toward the road with the thick mud grabbing and pulling at our feet. The water buffalos stood dumb-founded and watched as we darted by. There were no guards in sight, but two headlights approached from around a bend in the road. We flattened ourselves against the mud in a ditch beside the road as an army truck rolled by, unaware of our presence.

At last we stood at the edge of the river, but a cold and terrifying feeling ran through me. We could be blown to bits any second, either by stepping on a mine, or by stepping within range of a machine gun hidden in the bushes. Only faith and prayer could see our fate as we waded out into the river and swam towards the Thai shore. My parents hummed in a quiet prayer to the spirits of our ancestors for protection and guidance. The soft chanting of their voices seemed to cast a spell on everything, as if controlling the rhythm of the river current. Holding our little heads above the water so we could breathe, I listened and imagined the voices of my great ancestors assuring us of a safe journey across the river.

Back on the Lao shore, everything was dark and still. We listened for the guns, but all was silent. Any moment I expected the shore behind us to erupt in gunfire, but nothing happened. We kept on fighting the slow current, and after a while I realized that I wasn't dead — neither drowned or blasted apart by bullets. We were in the water for three hours before the current fi-

nally washed us up on a soft, sandy Thai beach.

We were free.

Looking back across the river and up towards the dim mountains of Laos on the other side, I felt I had left something terrible behind. I knew I had left my country. I had left the fear of death. But the memories of my village, the journey through the jungle, and the final crossing will always stay with me, if not haunt me. My sickness and near death in the Refugee Camps in Thailand shortly thereafter had a profound effect on how I longed to come to America. I had heard that others in the camp were going to the "USA." I wanted to attend school, but there was none in the camp. Soon, we were accepted to come to the United States, and I was sent to school starting in the fourth grade. I became a Boy scout

and graduated from college. I am becoming "American," and can finally live in the freedom that could never have been foreseen from the other side of the river. ▼

■ *The Mekong River flows out of Tibet and through the mountains of southern China, forming the boundary between Laos and Thailand. (Photo by Dave Moore).*

107

Boy Scouts

Dave Moore

■ *A Boy Scout leader and former teacher at Edison High School in Minneapolis, Dave authored the book "Dark Sky Dark Land, Stories of the Hmong Boy Scouts of Troop 100."*

In the Spring of 1981, a Boy Scout official asked me if I would teach a lesson in Scouting to the Hmong boys and girls at Edison High School in Minneapolis, where I was teaching. That first lesson was for me the start of a journey that changed my life, because as a result of it I became the Scoutmaster of Hmong Boy Scout Troop 100. Over the past twelve years, the Hmong Scouts and I have had a lot of fun together. We gave gone camping summer and winter; we have gone rock-climbing, white-water canoeing and skiing; we have learned the secrets of reflector-oven cooking and sampled such weird American foods as pancakes. We have braved the Boundary Waters and the snows of Minnesota. Many a time my mouth has watered as I looked forward to an evening meal of rice, fresh-caught fish, noodles and stir-fried vegetables. Twenty-eight of our boys have become some of the first Hmong Eagle Scouts in history.

There are currently over one hundred Scouts in Troop 100. Some of them arrived in America as recently as 1992, and a few were born in this country. Scouting is a way for them to improve their English, learn more about America, and keep in touch with their Hmong roots. Most Scouts tend to stay with the

" . . . Boy Scout Troop 100, sponsored by Westminster Church, was founded in 1980 with the aim of introducing Hmong boys to scouting and to American life and culture, and to help them learn English as they worked through the Scouting requirements. Our meetings, campouts and other activities have always been lively and well-attended, as the boys have discovered in the Troop a home where they can relax and enjoy themselves with Hmong friends We have gone camping, canoeing, rock climbing, swimming and skiing. We have conducted service projects for the Hmong community and for the community at large. We have learned about America from speakers, through field trips, and from working on Scout badges. We appear regularly at the Hmong New Year celebration, where we tell the story of scouting and what it can do for Hmong boys. Several of our members have attended national and world Boy Scout Jamborees. Twenty-seven have earned the Eagle rank.. "

—*Troop 100 Annual Report, 1993*

program for many years. Over 20 former Scouts who are now adults help the Troop on a regular or occasional basis. Last year, Eagle Scout Xia Thao received the Hiawatha District Award of Merit, given each year to an adult who performs outstanding service to Boy Scouts and to the community.

Here is how some of our boys feel about Scouting:

Chan Chang, Eagle Scout, Student at Brown Institute: "If it wasn't for Scouts, I'd just sit home and wouldn't know anything. Life would be tougher if there wasn't Boy Scouts."

Yupheng Vu, Eagle Scout, Student at the University of Minnesota: "I learned about my own culture in Troop 100. We made Hmong tops and pop guns and played Hmong games. I never knew how to do those things until I joined Scouts."

Su Thao, Eagle Scout, Graduate of Augsburg College: "You feel great about yourself because you're part of a group that can overcome obstacles. You get confidence to go out and meet challenges."

Yee Chang, Eagle Scout, Graduate of St. Olaf College: "The Hmong Troop is important to the Hmong community. It gives them a chance to see what their children have learned in America. It says to everyone, the Hmongs can accomplish something in America, as Hmongs." ▼

The Troop leader

A description of Scout leader Dave Moore as written by Tong Thao.

From the outside, Mr. Moore's

■ *Members of Boy Scout Troop 100 with U.S. Senator Paul Wellstone at the Minneapolis opening of the Center for Victims of Torture. (Photo by Dan Hess)*

109

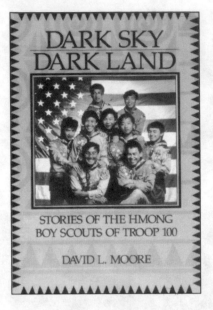

DARK SKY
DARK LAND

STORIES OF THE HMONG
BOY SCOUTS OF TROOP 100

DAVID L. MOORE

■ *Dave Moore wrote the book Dark Sky Dark Land about the experiences of his Hmong Boy Scouts.*

house looked like any other American house: a mail box in front of the door, a doorbell, and a doorknob. But inside, the place was a museum filled with all kinds of crafts, sculptures and pictures of people hung all around the living room and upstairs into the bedrooms. These pictures might seem strange if you didn't know the people in them. Among these people might be those you had met or seen somewhere but didn't really want to know or were afraid to approach. If you hadn't seen Mr. Moore in some time, you might think you were in the wrong house as many of the pictures are new. There are pictures of his fellow Scouts as well as those who had been his Scouts going back many years. They are all his friends.

When first entering Mr. Moore's house, you see a Japanese poster hung by a closet near the kitchen. As you turn towards the left, there is a table covered with scouting stuff: compasses, orienteering maps, a bugle, an American flag, merit badges, and pictures of boy scouts engaged in many activities. At the far end of the room are sculptures of animals and objects from other parts of the world and

still more pictures of Boy Scouts hung from the walls. Turning 180 degrees and walking towards the television, you see a picture of Mr. Moore himself standing in front of a famous old bus which goes on every trip the Boy Scouts take. On the walls close to the ceiling hang pictures of fifteen Hmong Eagle Scouts. On the left, a huge blanket of Hmong embroidery adorns the wall. The embroidery, called "Pa ndau," is inscribed with pictures telling a famous Hmong story about a tiger who ate a family one by one until he was killed by the last surviving daughter. Also inscribed on the blanket is a dramatic event: the escape of Hmong people from Laos to Thailand and then to the United States during the Vietnam War. And again, everywhere you turn is a picture of a Hmong Boy Scout posing with Mr. Moore.

Mr. Moore was born in 1936 in Minneapolis, Minnesota. The youngest of three boys, Mr. Moore and his two older brothers got involved in scouting because of their father. Mr. Moore's father wanted his boys to be Scouts because he valued the camping experience, though he wasn't a camper himself. He had had enough of it as a soldier in the First World War. Mr. Moore went on to become a Cub Scout in 1945 and an Eagle Scout in 1954.

Mr. Moore went to Fulton Elementary School and Southwest High School. Then in 1959, he graduated with bachelors and masters degrees from Yale University after

110

only five years of study. He taught Social Studies from 1959 to 1990.

Because Mr. Moore was an Eagle Scout, he was asked to become a Scoutmaster for the kids in Spring Valley, Minnesota. He taught and became a Scoutmaster at Spring Valley for a couple years. Then he went on to teach at a suburban school in Chicago.

"It was an interesting experience for me to teach in a small town like Spring Valley, because I had never lived in a small town before," said Mr. Moore. After teaching in suburban Chicago for a year, he went to Germany and taught at a U.S. Army base. Then in 1963, Mr. Moore returned to Minneapolis where he taught and took over Troop 33 as their Scoutmaster. Troop 33 was the troop in which Mr. Moore received his Eagle rank when he was young.

One day in January of 1981, while Mr. Moore was teaching at Edison High School, he saw hundreds of Hmong students walking around the school. They looked confused and didn't seem to know any English; they would just look down at the floor, speechless and lost. Because Mr. Moore was both a Scoutmaster and a teacher, the local Boy Scout office called on him to ask if he would organize a meeting for the Hmong students. The meeting turned into the beginning of Troop 100.

"Scouting was a good way to help them learn the American culture," said Mr. Moore.

Although the Hmong students

couldn't understand any English, they were able to figure out what Mr. Moore was trying to say whenever he demonstrated it to them instead of just talking. For example, when playing a game, he would demonstrate it as well as talk about it, and pretty soon one of the Hmong kids would figure out what he was trying to say. Whoever figured it out would explain it in Hmong to the others.

After many years of scouting with these Hmong boys, Mr. Moore found out that they had been part of the Vietnam War, some as soldiers fighting against the Communists. Because of this, he became convinced that American kids should know what these Hmong kids had gone through. He also thought the Hmong needed to let others know as part of getting beyond that miserable experience they had gone through. He decided to write a book about the lives of these young Hmong scouts. The book, titled "Dark Sky Dark Land," summed up these Hmong scouts'

■ Dave Moore traveled to Thailand to familiarize himself with his Hmong scouts' experience

111

lives.

After years of camping and coordinating Troop 100, Mr. Moore was given a Hmong name by his Hmong scouts. He was called "Seng Sue Moua," which means teacher.

Upon hearing the stories of how hard the boys' lives were and the difficulties they had encountered in Laos and the refugee camps of Thailand, Mr. Moore decided to visit the refugee camps for himself. He made an initial trip without a guide or interpreter, but it didn't satisfy his curiosity.

"I felt like I learned a lot more about who my kids were and where they had come from," said Mr. Moore after visiting camp Ban Vinai." Now I had to come back with a Hmong kid who could be my guide and introduce me to some of these people."

Two years later, in 1989, Mr. Moore returned to Thailand with Yee Chang one of his scouts who had lived in Ban Vinai. They met Yee's relatives who were still living there. The relatives didn't recognize Yee at first, but after a little while hundreds began gathering. They talked continuously for three days, asking Yee about America. Yee, in turn, asked them about their lives, and Mr. Moore was moved by the whole experience.

Mr. Moore travelled a third time to Thailand when Yee was there finishing his term as an exchange student at Chaing Mai University. The two visited fourteen Hmong villages, and Mr. Moore had the chance to sleep in several of them. At night they would all gather around a huge bonfire where Mr. Moore would tell stories with Yee translating and vice versa.

Mr. Moore is still Scoutmaster of both troop 100 and troop 33. One of the first things that comes to mind when he thinks about Troop 100 are the qualities of the Hmong kids. They seemed to live the Scout Law, with characteristics similar to its major points of trustworthiness, loyalty and bravery.

One of the most memorable trips Mr. Moore can remember having was when he went canoeing in Canada with some of the leaders of Troops 100 and 33. North of Winnipeg, they spent seven days continuously paddling and portaging across swamps and land areas. It was a real test of strength and endurance. Mr. Moore explained that Hmong kids liked to fish and camp – the kinds of things that scouts did. They didn't get to do these things in the city as much as the would like to. After over ten years with Troops 33 and 100, Mr. Moore hoped to keep doing these things with his scouts.

Mr. Moore retired from teaching at Minneapolis' Edison High School in 1990 because he felt the responsibilities of scouting were overwhelming him. Now he spends most of his time doing what he'd always wanted to do. He puts it this way, "It's neat to be working, but not for pay. The work somehow is more meaningful that way."

Twelve years ago, Mr. Moore felt

that after a couple of years, there wouldn't be a need for Troop 100. But now he senses there's even more need for it with Hmong kids having trouble living in two worlds – their parents' Hmong world and America's world of education. They need Troop 100 because they can be with their Hmong friends, speaking and doing Hmong things as well as American things. They can learn about both cultures while also being rescued from trouble. Mr. Moore strongly stated his belief that there would continue to be an indefinite need for Troop 100.

Though he doesn't know what his future holds, Mr. Moore will take what comes just as he took the reins of Troop 100. He enjoys watching kids grow up, especially scouts.

"They come to me as little eight-year old kids," he says, "and they grow into these fine young men who go out into the world and do stuff that I could never do." ▼

The Hmong

Scoutmaster Dave Moore gave his impressions of the young Hmong men who became an important part of his life as members of Troop 100.

My life started when I fell off a dock in northern Minnesota. The water was way over my head, and I remember sinking into the darkness of the lake, looking up and watching daylight slowly diminish above me as I sank. My two brothers fished me out. They built a big fire to dry me out and warm me up. I

was three years old.

I grew up with a fear of water, but I've always been drawn to it. Canoeing in Canada, I've swung my canoe broadside against angry waves, turning to help someone in trouble. I've battled torrential rains and sunk on lakes with weird Indian names. Through it all, I never lost my respect for water or my fascination with it.

Perhaps this is what first drew me to the Hmong students who showed up at Edison High School when I was teaching there in 1981. They too had had a rendezvous with water. They owed their lives to the crossing of a river of war: the

■ *A part of life in Laos, Hmong boys find outdoor activities an attractive feature of Scouting. Here Kao Vang and Kou Meng Lor examine shish kabobs cooked over an open fire (photo by Tom Hess).*

113

Mekong. By whatever means they could command – fishing boats, canoes, bamboo rafts, inner tubes or just swimming – they had done the impossible. Under fire, with only a shred of hope that there would be any kind of life for them on the other side, they had journeyed to freedom.

I respected them, and they became my good friends because, like me, they had survived.

▼▼▼

One time not long ago when I happened to be at Yee Chang's house over the noon hour, he invited me to stay for lunch. There was a large pot of chicken stewing on the stove. Yee fished around in the pot with a long spoon and came up with the chicken's head. He presented it to me with a grin and the statement, "Here, Dave, negative calories."

While Yee and his sister and brothers watched, I tried to gnaw the skin off the head. But then he showed me how to eat it: You crack it in your teeth like a walnut and suck the brains out. It didn't taste that bad, but there wasn't much there: chickens don't have the brains of Einstein. Anyway, how to eat a chicken head is one of many, many things I have learned from Yee over the last ten years.

One day in 1982, I think it was, a skinny little kid named Yee Chang showed up at a meeting of the Hmong Boy Scout Troop I had organized in Minneapolis. He had

seen us Scouts at our outdoor meetings at Stewart Park and he wanted to put on that snappy uniform with its blue-and-gold neckerchief and bright red epaulettes. So I met him. His friend said, "Dave, this is Yee." I said, "Hi, Yee." We shook hands. He seemed unable to speak much English, but he gave me a nice smile.

At first he was just another nice little Hmong kid, as far as I could tell, indistinguishable from dozens of others I knew. I hardly noticed him. But one night when we were on a Boy Scout overnight, Yee and I found ourselves sitting up late at a campfire, after everyone else had gone off to bed in their tents. The fire was almost out. There was a fall chill in the air and no moon. I wasn't thinking about anything, just staring into the embers, when Yee suddenly made a remark. "I've seen a lot of first aid," he said.

We had been working on first aid earlier that afternoon and he must have been thinking about that. But what did he mean? There was something hushed and distant in his voice, as if he were speaking from far away in some other world. I looked at him, and it was as if I was really seeing him for the first time.

"What did you say?" I asked.

He repeated, "I've seen a lot of first aid."

His form was indistinct in the darkness. I squinted at him. "What do you mean? What are you talking about?"

And out came a story of a far-away world destroyed by war, of head-long flight, of days and nights of running, of near starvation and surrender, of escape and rescue and fire-fights and near drowning in a great river, of sickness and near death in a refugee camp, and finally a long journey to a new land and a new chance at life. It was a story told in that totally honest, unembellished, matter-of-fact way that is so familiar to anyone who knows Yee: He wasn't trying to impress me, he was just telling me, because I had asked.

But I was impressed. I was moved as I have never been before or since.

I have done a lot of things with Yee over the years. I've traveled with him to Washington, D.C. to be interviewed on CNN, and to Kansas City to organize a Hmong Boy Scout Troop. We've gone canoeing deep in Canada three or four times. For about five summers, he has been the Program Director for the younger guys, age eight to eleven, at Camp Ajawah, which I direct. I helped him to become one of America's first Hmong Eagle Scouts and I talked him into entering the Hmong Teenager of the Year contest, which he won. I wrote a book about him and his Hmong buddies. He is an important part of who I am and an influence on what I do. And it's all because of a campfire story — a story that changed my life in ways I am only just beginning to understand.

▼▼▼

On being a Boy Scout

Following are accounts of scouting given by Hmong members of Boy Scout Troop 100.

■ Yer Yang

I was born in a small village in Laos in 1976. When I was three years old, we had to leave Laos because of the war. My mom, my little brother and I had to swim across the Mekong River to Thailand. I could not swim, so I had to hang onto my mom.

We stayed in a camp in Thailand for nine months and then came to America. My first memory of America is being in school. I had to go to the bathroom all day, but I didn't know how to ask, so I had to wait till I got home.

In the spring of 1989, my friend, Toua Vue, told me to join the Boy Scouts. I decided to give it a shot. I will always remember my first camping trip. I was not prepared. I was too cold. I wished I was home. But I learned how to keep warm.

That summer I went to Camp Ajawah. I learned how to swim and how to save myself from drowning. Last summer I was a counselor at Ajawah. Now I am an Eagle Scout and the Senior Patrol Leader of Troop 100. I like being a Scout. It's fun. You learn about yourself. You learn that you can do anything if you try hard enough.

Because I joined Scouts I can swim, I can take care of myself in the outdoors, I can get a bunch of kids to listen to me and do what I tell them, I can stand up and talk to

Moo Vu
■ *Moo is a Boy Scout in Troop 100.*

Yimeem Vu
■ *Yimeem is a member of Troop 100.*

116

a group of people.

That's what being a Scout has done for me. ▼

■ Yimeem Vu (Interviewed by Moo Vu)

To me, Boy Scouts is about learning how to live in the wilderness. I joined because I wanted to learn how my family had lived. In Thailand and Laos, they had to learn to live by themselves in the wilderness. But I wouldn't know what to do if I went back to Laos someday because I was born in the United States. I'm just a city boy, and I don't know what to do in the wilderness.

We do lots of stuff in Boy Scouts. We go camping, play games and work on ranks that help us learn different skills. The Troop meets at Westminster Presbyterian Church in downtown Minneapolis every Friday. I'm a Star Scout in Troop 100 working on a Life rank. The highest rank is Eagle, and you can go past that to get your Eagle palms. But I think an even higher rank is becoming a scoutmaster.

I think Boy Scout Troop 100 affects the Hmong people because it gives kids a place to turn to get away from gangs. They don't have to always be in a bad environment.

We usually go camping on weekends during both the winter and summer. Our leader decides where. Every winter we sell grapefruits, oranges, apples and pears to raise money for these trips.

There are over twenty Eagle Scouts in Troop 100. I'm pretty sure I'm going to be an Eagle Scout too someday – at least, I hope to be one. But I don't know about taking over the Troop or starting a new one. I don't think that's going to be in my future.

I found out about scouting from my brother Yu Pheng. He became an Eagle Scout, and I went to his ceremony. My cousin and I decided we were going to have a race to see who got Eagle rank first. That's how I started in Boy Scouts.

I'm very proud to be a Boy Scout. Though a lot of people would laugh and say I shouldn't be proud of being Boy Scout, I would gladly say that I am proud of what I can and have accomplished through Scouting.

There are four parts of the Scout Law that I like and hope to carry on: being trustworthy, loyal, helpful and courteous. If you can't be trusted, that's the end of your reputation– no one can depend on you. Loyalty is like trustworthiness. I like to help out where help is needed, because if everyone isn't helpful, people would be greedy. Nobody would get anything done. Courtesy is just plain good manners. It's knowing what to do and when to do it without embarrassing others; it's showing respect. ▼

■ Paul Yang

One thing that happened that changed my life a little was joining the Boy Scouts. My life was a normal, everyday life until I joined Boy Scouts. Since joining, I've made many friends. I've also

learned many things, for example: how to cook better; how to get along with other people; skills like hiking, camping, building a fire, canoeing, swimming and fishing. I've earned merit badges and ranks, becoming more responsible and gaining leadership skills in the process. I hope to be a good role model and make myself a better person so that people can really understand me and not simply confuse me with my appearance. Joining Boy Scouts got my life on track.

We've done many other neat and exciting things in Boy Scouts. We've gone camping, hiking, fishing, biking, rollerskating, swimming, and exploring dams and mines. We've played football in both the grass and the snow.

The most challenging activity for me was a canoe trip to Woodland Caribou, a park around the Manitoba-Ontario border. One straight week of canoeing, going through portages ranging from the maximum of tow miles to about 10-15 yards. It was hard carrying 70 pounds on your back while going through these portages, but the trip was fun and adventurous.

Joining Boy Scouts has also helped me deal with problems I face often: anger, frustration, decision-making and pain. Scouting has helped me learn to respect and help people outside of my race. I feel that I should never judge a person by their nationality or race, but by who they are inside. ▼

■ *Lined up in the top photo are (L-R) Kou Vue, Song Neng Lee, Dave Moore, Xoua Pha. Travis Zorn and Yee Chang, Eagle Scouts from Dave Moore's two Boy Scout Troops (courtesy of Westminster Church).*

117

Trustworthy, Loyal and Brave

■ *Boy Scout Troop 100 was started in 1981. Pictured above are Scoutmaster Dave Moore, Va Vang, Doua Xiong, Koua Her and Kao Vang (photo courtesy of Paul Irmiter) and young scouts listened intently at a weekly Troop meeting (Courtesy of Larry Roepke).*

■ *Boy Scouts enjoy blue berries along portage trails in the deep woods of Canada (photo by Dan Hess).*

■ *Va Vang dries clothes over a fire. Above, Tong Thao, Toua Vue and Yer Yang display their catch in Woodland Caribou Provincial Park (photos by Dan Hess).*

119

16 Caught Between Cultures

■ *A young Hmong girl at the New Year Celebration in St. Paul peers out from between two cultures. (Photo by Dan Hess)*

There are three kinds of Hmong young people. I call them the American-Hmongs, the Hmong-Americans, and the Rebels. The American-Hmongs are trying to achieve the American definition of success. They are trying to make it in America, and to make it in American terms. But nevertheless they cling to their Hmong loyalty and identity. On the other hand, the Hmong-Americans are trying to achieve the Hmong definition of success. They are trying to make it in America, and to make it in Hmong terms. They, too, cling to their Hmong loyalty and identity. Finally, the Rebels are in revolt against their Hmong identity. They tend to reject everything that strikes them as Hmong, and instead they grasp what in their view is the American culture. But what they strive to adopt usually turns out to be a caricature of the American culture and not the real thing.

The American-Hmong is a person caught between two cultures. In his striving for success in America, he has accepted numerous and intense pressures. First, he has the internalized pressure of trying to force himself to learn the American language and culture. The oral skills of a Hmong college student

120

may be excellent. He may speak English with little or no accent. But his written work is much more difficult. He has trouble with plurals and tense. And there are great gaps in his fund of background knowledge. Finally, Hmong people do not necessarily think in the same way that Americans think. "I study all night for a test. I memorize all the facts and have them all in my mind. When I see the test, the questions are all familiar and I know the answers, but I can't give the right answers to the questions." Many students respond in this way to their studies. Failure here may be caused by a lack of skill in reading English and interpreting questions, a lack of background knowledge, panic brought on by lack of self-confidence, or thought-processes which are not congenial to an American college exam. Whatever the cause of difficulty, college is a struggle, with Hmong students competing at a disadvantage with their American colleagues. Whatever time an American student spends studying, Hmong students feel they have to double that just to stay even in what they see as a highly competitive situation. Goals and expectations are high, and results can be discouraging and even devastating. Reality catches up to many Hmong students in college and they find themselves changing their career goals from doctor, lawyer or engineer to more realistic but less prestigious goals such as social worker or elementary-school teacher. Or, they may drop out of college entirely, although most are willing to continue the struggle. Their faith is that by hard work and persistence they can succeed. And success in college is essential to their future role in family and clan. It is important to have a well-paying job, but prestige is an even more important goal than wealth.

A second kind of pressure on the American-Hmong is the pressure put on him by family and clan elders. These are his parents, grandparents, aunts and uncles. They have made the long journey from the refugee camps in Thailand in order to give their children a future. In America, they are counting on their children to pull them out of poverty. Raised in the Hmong tradition of total respect amounting to reverence for their elders, the American-Hmong youth feel a tremendous responsibility to live up to the elders' expectations of them. The elders point to the young American-Hmong as a role model for dozens of younger siblings, cousins, nieces and nephews.

However, the pressure to succeed in America as an American is not the only pressure that the young Hmong gets from his elders, because at the same time that they are urging him to succeed in school, they are urging him to be a good Hmong and to fulfill his obligations as an adult or near-adult Hmong. This may involve attending family and clan ceremonies, taking care of small children, getting a part-time job to support himself and the family, getting married and having children of his own. The elders do not always understand the inherent contradiction between the American student life-style with its demands on a person's time and energy, and the "good Hmong" life style with its demands. The result is that the Hmong youth constantly finds himself in situations in which he has to decide whether to respond as a Hmong or as an American. Should he join the school soccer team and risk breaking his ankle in play? How important is soccer to his education? Does he want to join the team just for fun and relaxation or is he doing it in order to learn and make valuable contacts? If his elders don't want him to join, should he respect their wishes, or should he try to talk them into letting him do it? And if he does argue with them, is he giving the real reasons or just rationalizing his desires?

Or, a Hmong boy wants to take his Hmong girl-friend to the school prom. What should he do? In the first place, proper Hmong boys don't have Hmong girl friends. But this is America, and things are a little different here. So the boy goes to the girl's parents, sits down with them and explains that the prom is a part of the school's program and hence a part of his and the girl's education. The parents listen and, somewhat confused, give their consent. The boy takes the girl to the prom. They enjoy the evening and have a good time together and with their school mates. But at the same time the boy feels guilty: Did he take advantage of the elders? Did he fool them into letting him do something they would never have approved of if they had fully understood what a prom was? One thing is certain: he has made their lives a little more complicated and less secure. He has challenged their authority and come off the winner, which was not his intention: he only wanted to take his girl friend to the prom. He feels badly about this. The Hmong boy envies his American friends who have no such difficulty in participating in such an ordinary American activity.

In addition to his elders, another group from whom the American-Hmong youth feels pressure is his Hmong peers. The more successful he appears to be, the more his peers will seek him out for advice, explanations, friendship. He may come home from college for a week-end break to find three or four of his friends who are struggling and perhaps floundering and who are seeking his understanding and support. Their own elders may not be in a good position to help them: too old, too poor, out of touch. A boy's parent may be a second wife, unable to stand up to a father who lives with his first, and preferred, wife. Cast adrift, these young men turn to the more successful of their peers for the support they need. The American-Hmong youth thus may spend most of his week-end "breaks" giving psychological band-ade council and support to his peers. On Monday, he returns to his school and to his own struggles with a mixed sense of exhaustion, relief and accomplishment. ▼

Living in the U.S.A.

By Dan Hess

On a seemingly insignificant Saturday afternoon in early spring 1982, I had my first meal in a Hmong home and my first lesson in Hmong hospitality – a meal and lesson I'll not soon forget.

The Hmong people had recently begun emigrating in large numbers to Minnesota, and I worked with a Scout Troop formed to help Hmong boys adapt to their new culture. Most of the Scouts spoke no English. We depended on those who could speak some English to help the Troop. One of our translators was a 13-year old boy named Chu.

Chu was a funny guy. He had a crooked smile that never completely disappeared, and his round head was balanced on a thin neck. He always wore his shirt buttoned to the collar, which had the effect of making his head appear larger and his neck appear thinner than they really were. His pants were too short, and he moved with a loose-jointed clumsiness. His voice squeaked and creaked like a rusty hinge, changing pitch with a vengeance. But despite his funny appearance, Chu was also one of the most gentle and friendly people I'd ever met.

Over time, I learned that neither of Chu's parents had survived the escape from Laos. He lived with an older brother and other members of his extended family in a crowded duplex in south Minneapolis not far from where we held our Troop meetings.

The Troop met on Fridays, the only meeting day the scouts felt wouldn't interfere with their homework. At the close of one meeting, Chu, with his typical smile and creaky voice, asked the Scoutmaster and me if we could visit him on Saturday for lunch at his house. We gladly accepted.

The next day we arrived at Chu's house about lunch time and knocked on the door. With a bigger than usual smile, Chu opened the door and waved us in. He took our coats, showed us into the living room, and invited us to be seated. The furnishings were spare; the house was neat, and I noticed it was very quiet. Where were the children and other relatives? We had the living room to ourselves as we looked at each other and talked.

Our conversation proceeded haltingly for several minutes until Chu produced a Monopoly gameboard and waited for our reaction. He wanted to play American, and this was evidently the most American thing he knew. So we all played Monopoly, with Chu as the race car, me as the shoe. We played and played, aware of the occasional face of a small child peering curiously around the door. After a moment, the wide-eyed little faces would retreat, the door would close, and we would hear laughter. The Monopoly game continued endlessly through the afternoon, becoming a marathon that no one could win –

Dan Hess
■ *Dan is Assistant Scoutmaster of Troop 100.*

123

Va Vang

■ *Va is an eighth grade student in Minneapolis and a Boy Scout in Troop 100.*

does anyone ever win at Monopoly?

Finally, various bowls of food began quietly appearing on the dining room table, and our game drew to a close. We walked to the table for a closer look and saw meat everywhere, roasted, boiled and fried. It was floating in soup, mixed with vegetable greens and cut into plain chunks. And there was rice. Someone set a glass of warm, green vegetable broth in front of my friend and me, but no one else had a beverage.

We sat at the table with a number of other men, but Chu stood behind us and watched attentively. Everyone's shirt was buttoned to the collar. Chu listened seriously when one of his relatives said something important. He would then lean his head in between my friend and me, smile, and explain in his broken English what had been said. He would then translate our words to the group.

Before we ate, Chu's brother wanted to tell a story. Chu translated as his brother told the American guests about the food on the table. He explained what was in each bowl, then told of the hunt from which the meat was obtained. Chu's brother spoke with pride as I watched. He had gone to Wisconsin to stalk his quarry in the early morning. Upon siting it in a field, he crept up along a fence to get a good shot and fired.

He had successfully hunted a cow!

My friend and I glanced at each other grinning silently. I looked at the roasted liver in front of me. Did Chu's brother really shoot a cow, or was it a deer? I didn't ask. The food was delicious, and we sat at the table for a long time talking and laughing.

I was recently invited to another such Hmong meal. I was seated politely and fed roasted meat and rice. But there was also turkey, stuffing, vegetable salads, hot dogs, doritos, cake and Mountain Dew. This time, only the old men spoke Hmong. The younger men spoke English, and the children wore designer clothes and played Nintendo games on the television. I thought of the monopoly game at Chu's house that first visit and how no one could ever win at Monopoly. The meal was over quickly here, and people were looking at their watches. It struck me how time had passed and a culture had evolved.

Monopoly always won. ▼

❝ What's it like to be a Hmong kid in America? ❞

■ Va Vang

Being a Hmong kid in America means having more chance of getting an education. I sometimes feel very sad about myself because I'm a Hmong kid. Why? Because Hmong is a group of people that have have only 2 to 3 million people, and we have no country which we can call Hmong land. In Ameri-

■ *Members of Troop 100 participating in HYCAP: Kao Vang, Va Vang, Paul Yang and Yimeem Vu. (Photo by Dan Hess)*

ca, learning English is the hardest thing for me. I think America is great. It has a beautiful sight of land and high buildings and the people are very nice. It is difficult to be a Hmong kid in America because I am caught between two cultures, Hmong and American. So, I think that it's not easy for me to follow my culture because I live in the American society. I have to learn Hmong and American culture at the same time. The reason I think that I have to learn both cultures is because both cultures are important to me. It will take me a while to learn the Hmong culture because I learn about American culture in school more than Hmong. But I am still interested in learning about Hmong culture and history. I still care about my Hmong people. Also, I still remember who I am.

Living in America is tough because you have to learn how to speak English. To me, speaking English is kind of tough because I usually can't pronounce some words clearly. Living in America is a main reason I came because of freedom. Two things I hate about America are that you have to follow their dumb laws, and people in America don't like us because we're Hmong. People think that we are just some bad Hmong people that settled in their country. To me the most prejudiced people are police, because they think they have the right to swear at us and other people such as blacks. I guess I will have to stick to my life as it is now. I can't just wait to go back where I belong. If people think that we should not settle in their country, I think we should not settle in their country, I think we shouldn't be in this stupid country. If people in America could just give us a chance they would probably learn more about our background. I know some people would like to learn about our culture. And I say that we shouldn't tell some of them because they probably don't deserve to know about our culture. Why can't we just get along? I never fit

125

in the crowds at school because they probably think I'm bad in some way. I hope in the future Americans would face us and know more about us. So, why can't we just get along, you people out there!

■ Paul Yang

It's hard living in America as a Hmong boy. It's especially hard in this country that's not ours feeling left out of the white community, hearing the things they say behind our backs. I'm not saying that all whites are bad, but some just change when they look at us. They see us as something less than who they are. I feel that life's sometimes harder because of the impact other races have on us.

The Hmong are members of a poor race, but we are hardworking and ambitious. In Laos we didn't achieve anything more than a good year's crop, but here in America we want to be on the same level of importance as other minority groups and the white group. The young kids don't quite understand the amount of frustration and confusion their parents have because of money problems, such as not making enough money to satisfy their needs. And that's why they put a lot of pressure on us kids, by telling us that whatever we do, no matter what, just work hard, get a good education, and we will have a good life and avoid the same hardships they had.

■ Chua Chang

It's pretty easy being a Hmong kid in America because I think life's easier here than in Thailand or Laos. I don't have to do things that are hard, like feeding the animals. And there, you don't have a lot of clothes to wear. Living in America is easy because you don't have to build your own house, you just rent or buy one.

■ Mai See Xiong

I think being a Hmong kid in America is good. Sometimes it can be bad, too. The bad part is that you have no freedom to do whatever you want, and parents are always in control. The good part is that you get to know more people from different cultures and learn about them. There is school for you and you get to learn. I think that being a Hmong kid in America is great, but not always.

■ Betty Chang

For me it's pretty easy being a Hmong kid in America because I don't feel different from other people or cultures. I get treated pretty equally by other people. When I am in school I don't feel very different because there are many other Hmong kids. But, once in a while, I don't want to be a Hmong. Sometimes I get mad at my culture because I don't think that males and females are treated equally. Sometimes a person from another culture makes fun of us, calls us Chinese, and tells us to go back to our country. Some times, they make fun of the way we talk in our language, and try to imitate us.

Mostly, it's easy being a Hmong, but sometimes I wish that I was from another culture. But, I'm still proud to be Hmong.

■ Pang Xiong

I am the only daughter in the family and I feel really bad because I have nobody to talk to. Sometimes when I 'm bored, or even when I'm desperate to talk to somebody, I can't express my feelings to anyone. And I feel sad because I don't have a sister to play with me.

Being the only girl in the family, I have a lot of responsibilities. If I don't do them, no one else will. My mom does most of the morning work and the weekend work. But when she's out of the house, I have to take care of everything. I am responsible for the house chores such as cooking, and cleaning. Sometimes, when I tell my father or brother to do the cooking and the dishes, they help. But usually when I won't cook, there's trouble and they give me a lecture. They say, "We are men, and you are the girl in the family and you are supposed to do the house chores."

When I'm doing my homework, I don't have time for chores. I think the parents should understand that if their son/daughter is working on their homework they should be allowed to study. And, since the parents expect their children to get good grades in every class, they shouldn't force their children to do other things when their mind is on homework. Sometimes when I'm studying, my parents ask me to do something for them. I try to explain everything to them , but they don't understand. So I have to finish what they had asked me to do before I can continue my schoolwork. By the time I finish their chore, my mind is on a totally different subject and I can't concentrate on my studies. Sometimes I have a hard time telling them not to ask me to do so many things at the same time.

▼ ▼ ▼

First day in school

By Bruce Xiang

My first day of school was awful because I couldn't find my classroom. I was frustrated and didn't know what to do in class because I didn't understand what the teacher was talking about. I had a hard time learning English because I had not studied it before I came to the United States. English is a language that has past tense and future tense, and many verbs, nouns, adjectives, adverbs, and prepositions. With so many things to learn, I was confused, even to learn basic English. But, now I love to learn English, and study as much as I can.

By Betty Chang

I go to Folwell Junior High and remember my first day in that school. When I first got there, I worried about not having any friends because I'm not a very outspoken person. I went to my advisory class which was in room 03. I saw a person that I knew from last school year and I was relieved. We started talking to each other and pretty soon became friends. I met a lot of other nice people so I didn't worry any more about not having friends, but I did worry about not fitting in. But, pretty soon I realized that I didn't really want to be in a group because I liked being by myself, and I'm not going to change the fact that I'm me for anything or anyone.

School turned out to be o.k., better than I had expected. We have a lot of writing-down things for tests, unlike elementary school. Sometimes I get a lot of homework when I'm feeling lazy, but I know that it is for my own good and education. I don't hang around with my friend as much as I used to, but she's still there when I need to talk to someone. School is getting better all the time even though it can be boring. I think that I am going to have a successful school year.

Racism

One day, as I was about to climb the outside stairs to the Vangs' apartment in Minneapolis, I encountered some teen-age American girls.

"Are you visiting 'Chinks'?" one of them asked, incredulous.

"No, I'm visiting friends," I replied. I stepped around her and started on up the steps without looking back.

In coming to America from a war of extermination in their homeland, the Hmong face an endemic racism in our society. They have potentially fallen heir to all the racial slurs and stereotypes applied to Asians since the first few Chinese forty-niners arrived in the gold fields of California.

But the racism that the Chinese encountered in California is really older than that: it goes back to some of the first encounters of Europeans with the racially "Other" in the sixteenth century. This initial meeting shaped all subsequent encounters. For example, the "racial science" of the nineteenth century and the images evoked by the U.S. war with Japan in the twentieth century, both reinforced the original stereotypes -- so that, in 1980, a Hmong family, stepping off an airplane into a Minnesota winter, was hit, not only by snow and cold, but by all of this accumulated racism, persisting essentially unchanged for five centuries. It is my contention here that the Asian-American experience of racism has been basically the same as that encountered by the Indians who met the first conquistadores.

It seems that in racial thought, nothing changes -- it just adapts. Whoever happens to be Other at any particular moment receives the whole burden of racial hatred. In the twentieth century came World War II, and another in the continuing series of violent encounters between the white and colored races. All of the old stereotypes were brought out of the centuries-old closet. The Japanese were apes, children, madmen. When the war ended in 1945, these images did not die. They were transformed and subsequently transferred to other, newer enemies: the Chinese and then the Vietnamese.

The Hmong in America today are the heirs of that long legacy of hostile images, a legacy not of their own making. The Hmong, like Indians, Africans and other Asians before them, have encountered the West in incredibly violent circumstances. During the Vietnam War, they were America's staunchest allies in Southeast Asia. We protected their mountain villages and sustained them with rice drops from airplanes. They, in turn, rescued downed American pilots deep within enemy territory. They manned electronic tracking stations that told our forces about enemy troop movements. But they paid a price for their allegiance.

In spite of the obviously strong affinity between the Hmong soldiers and the American pilots, a good case could be made that the Americans used the Hmong, just as they had earlier exploited black slave labor, and as the Spanish had exploited Indian labor.

The America that the Hmong entered in 1980 was a different place from the America of the Second World War and earlier. Just as the Civil War became a war to free the slaves, the Second World War be-

came a war against racism. Out of it came the civil rights revolution and the apology to Japanese-Americans for their mistreatment here at home during the war.

Overt racism is not tolerated in the U.S. today. No one debates the "nature" of the Hmong. As resident aliens, they have all the rights of any other resident. Some have become citizens by naturalization, and many of their children have been born here and so are citizens by birth.

If not overt, racism has a way of turning covert. A white student in a schoolroom whispers to a Hmong boy, "Hey, kid, do you eat cat?" Behind the intended insult is a real question: How different are you?

But there is something else in the Hmong's situation. They find themselves in the 1990's part of a new phenomenon, 'the model minority.' Hardworking, ambitious, loyal and totally reliable, they have earned universal respect. This puts them in jeopardy, because now they are a model -- for whom? That there is a model minority implies that there are other minorities that are not models, that fall short of the ideal, that need to be instructed. And it's not hard to find those 'other' minorities.

And so the Hmong, along with all other Asian-Americans, find themselves square in the middle of the old racial antagonism between African-Americans and European-Americans, Native-Americans and European-Americans. But this, too, is not new. The first Chinese immi-

129

grants in the West found themselves being used by white employers to drag down wages for all workers, and so caught in the middle of a labor war between social classes. Yesterday's 'coolie' is today's model minority.

This is particularly distressing for the Hmong because, while intelligent enough and willing to work, they have little or no formal educational background. Those graduating now from college are the first generation to do so. The idea that the Hmong must be brilliant scholars just because they are Asian, is too much for some. They give up and drop out.

The burden of racism, inherited from the European-American past is only one of the many burdens the Hmong have to bear. Families are fragmented. Material resources are near zero. Children and parents are drifting further and further apart as the Western culture, all but incomprehensible to the old, attracts the young. As the Hmong struggle to rebuild shattered lives in this country, racism is something they do not need, or deserve.

The gang problem

Illustration by Paul Yang

By Doua Chang

Since Hmong people settled in the United States, they have faced many problems. These problems come from trying to adjust to American culture. For adults, the main problem is learning English. It is hard for them because they are old and can't learn as quickly. The young have other problems, some so difficult to deal with that they feel like giving up.

Growing up in urban America is very hard, especially for Hmong youth. I was fortunate to have a strong family who never gave up in trying to keep me from trouble. With many Hmong kids joining or becoming affiliated with gangs, some are becoming violent and committing crimes. Others just want to hang out with friends. Yet all are being labeled as "gang bangers." In the eyes of elders, they are all bad.

Why do kids join gangs? Parents struggled so hard to get to this country so their children could have a better life. Yet for the many reasons that Hmong youth join gangs, it is often because of family problems.

I had the opportunity of talking with a teenager who had such problems. I'll call him "PV." He was a former a gang member who had come to the U.S. when he was six years old. When his family arrived here, they moved into the predominantly Hmong McDonough Housing Project in St. Paul. PV was responsible for his three younger siblings. He was harassed at school and often picked on at home.

"Being the oldest ain't easy," he told me. "My mom wanted me to do everything, but I couldn't."

When he reached Junior High, PV began to steal and smoke. His mom hated it when he would smoke around the house, but he didn't care. Communication between him and his parents soon deteriorated. They couldn't understand one another. PV became angry and frustrated with them and with himself. He decided to join a gang, and things started falling apart.

"When I think about it now, " he admits, "it was dumb of me. But it was the easy way out."

Many Hmong youths who have problems at home don't know what to do because their parents can't understand where they're coming from. Sometimes the teenager just needs to get away and be with people who make them feel wanted. They go to their peers for support and often join gangs. All they have is each other. It's like a second fami-

■ Paul Yang

I think gangs are dumb. The things they do are stupid. You don't get anything when you join a gang. You only get into trouble with people who you think are your friends. Then they're not your friends, anymore.

ly, a group of friends who help and look out for one another.

Hmong youths often feel that their parents don't encourage, support or even care about what they do. They often join gangs because they don't get enough attention from parents, teachers and other adult figures. In some cases, they don't have any adult figure or role model to look up to. Young people need attention and good role models. They need to feel wanted and to have a sense of belonging. They need somebody to show them they have many choices, not just one or two.

Many Hmong youths feel stressed as a result of keeping everything to themselves. Some may not be doing well in school. They reach a point where they just don't care anymore. There has to be a person or place where they can get help. They turn to their peers when they can't get help from adults, because the people who have been through the same experiences are going to understand them.

Gangs have a great impact on the Hmong and on the larger community. The rise in Hmong gang activity has begun to frighten many elders. This fear has resulted in many precautions in staging major Hmong events such as the New Year celebration or annual Soccer Tournament. Security is tight. Sometimes people with outrageous clothes or hair styles become the targets of suspicion, and events that are supposed to bring the Hmong community together for a good time often end with some sort of gang-related violence. People have become afraid to attend even parties for fear of a fight or shooting.

Though not all gang members are bad, they carry a negative image. You may see them hanging around street corners or roaming the malls, yet few people care to ask them why. They don't know what kinds of problems these kids have at home; maybe they don't want to know. People only look at idle Hmong youth with disgust and walk away. Some of these kids who are just hanging around would really like something more constructive to do in a place where they feel wanted.

There is a solution to getting kids off gangs, but it takes time and commitment. The community needs to take a look at the problems that teenagers face and help them find alternatives. Parents should teach and discipline their kids at a young age and provide them with enough understanding and freedom to grow. Because a lot of the problems start at home, parents must create a caring and loving en-

vironment there.

Youths must want to change. They must realize the hardships their parents went through to get them where they are and provide them with a good education. They need to develop self esteem instead of relying on their peers all the time. And they need to become independent – working to get what they want instead of taking the easy way out. The "easy way" might get them a ticket to trouble or even death.

I've had some experience with gangs, and from what I know, Hmong gangs appeared just a few years ago in the late 1980s. I think that Hmong gangs are tearing up our community, making all of us look bad. Now there are even Hmong on Hmong crimes because of the gangs. This is very disturbing. If we pull together and are dedicated enough to make a difference, we can stop gangs from taking away our Hmong teenagers. We are a small community. If we want to be strong, we have to stick together.

By Doua Chang

All through my grade school years and in junior high, I had a best friend. His name was Moua. We lived in the same neighborhood, went everywhere and did everything together. We went biking, roller skating, swimming, everything, together. Back in those days it was just me and him. It seemed like nothing could stop us. We thought we were on the roll.

Doua Chang

■ *Doua is a sophomore at South High School in Minneapolis.*

132

We'd been through good and bad times together, and through it all we learned a lot of things. Then, one day he moved away, to live in south Minneapolis. He then started hanging around with the wrong people, and started doing bad things. I told him to come to South High with me, but he went to Edison High, instead. He barely went to school the entire first year. I then realized how much Moua had changed. By the end of the school year, Moua had practically dropped out of school and started working at McDonald's. We never hung out together like we used to in the old days, but I knew he still had that side to him, the old side that I missed.

Before I could talk to him again, I learned that he got locked-up. I don't know the reason, but I know that he was to be locked up for a couple of months. When people tell me about him, they always just shake their head in disappointment. I received a letter from him just recently and he filled me in on how he was doing. I read his letter and it sounded like the old Moua I used to know in grade school.

It's weird how some people change so quickly, and don't realize it until it's too late.

By Kao Vang

In 1987, I was playing in a park in north Minneapolis when I saw some Hmong guys cleaning up the park. I asked them what they were doing. They said they were Boy Scouts doing a service project. An American guy who was with them came up to me and asked if I wanted to be Boy Scout. I said, "Sure." I joined Hmong Boy Scout Troop 100 and have been part of it ever since. Being in 100 has taught me a lot of things. I learned how to cook, go camping, tie knots and swim.

Last summer we went on a canoe trip in Canada. On the last day of the trip, we were cold, soaking wet and tired. I didn't have a rain coat, so I tried to stay warm by running around, singing songs and keeping active, but Dave, our Scoutmaster, said I was crazy. He said I was going to freeze to death. So we stopped, unpacked our bags and shared out all our dry clothes. We built a fire out of the wind and made lunch. After that everything was fine.

There is no doubt in my mind that Troop 100 kept me out of trouble. Some Hmong kids who have nothing to do after school are getting into trouble. Some of them join gangs. They break the law. But I was lucky. I joined Troop 100. If I had not joined Troop 100, I can't imagine what I'd be doing right now. Scouting is a big part of my life. All my friends are Scouts. If I wasn't a Scout, I know I'd be in a gang causing trouble. My relationship with my parents would be dif-

■ *Kao Vang, Senior Patrol Leader in Troop 100, made this short speech before the assembly of Westminster Presbyterian Church in Minneapolis, Minnesota. The occasion was Scout Sunday, March 6, 1994.*

ferent, and I would be behind in all my school work. Troop 100 has kept me on the right path. Troop 100 has given me the opportunity of my life.

▼ ▼ ▼

My Parents

By Doua Chang

It was the winter of 1988, and I was about 10 years old. I remember vaguely what happened on the second day of the year, something that changed my life forever.

My cousins in St. Paul were having a New Year's Party, and everyone in my family went, except my dad and my step mother. I remember getting bundled up for the cold weather, and then getting dropped off at my cousin's house. There, I saw all my friends, and did what I usually do. We had our own little party. We drank pop, watched movies, and played games. It seemed like any other old-people party. Then the phone rang and I overheard some old folks saying something about my dad. I didn't know what, but it didn't seem good. My sister walked over to me with a strange look on her face, a face that I had never seen before, and said, "Dad's dead." I was frozen for a second and couldn't speak. I was still young, and I didn't know exactly what was happening.

My sister and I were rushed to the hospital, immediately. Our cousins were already there, and I

still wasn't sure what was happening. All I knew was that everyone was crying. I walked around the lobby a bit confused until I saw one of my brothers. He picked me up and held me, and cried harder than I'd ever seen him cry before. He kept saying, "Dad's dead, Doua, Dad's dead." I didn't know what to do or say but to cry along with him. It was the strangest feeling I've ever had, and I didn't understand it. But I knew that I was scared, and my dad was gone, forever.

> ❝ Sometimes I want to tell my parents. ❞

■ Tong Thao

Sometimes I want to tell my parents that I love them. Although they've never told me straight that they love me, I know that they do. I sometimes wonder why parents in my culture never tell their children how much they love them. Maybe its because they have never said it, and if they do, they would be too embarrassed. I hope someday to be different than my parents. I wish I could tell my parents how much I love them, but I hope they already know. Sometimes I have dreams of telling my parents that I love them, but when I wake up, its only a dream. I love my parents even though I could never tell them. I've never said it. I'm too embarrassed and maybe they are, too.

■ Alee Chang

Through childhood, I've always felt responsible and always having to do most of the things around the house because I'm the oldest of six children. Well, I didn't get much freedom either, having to take care of my sisters and brothers. And doing most of the house work.

School went through good. I was a good student, not exactly great, but all right.

Sometimes I want to tell my parents about how I really feel. But I guess it's kind of hard for me to have a close relationship. I want to be able to talk to my mom comfortably and tell her secrets, like she was my best friend. I know I'll never be able to have that kind of friendship with them for as long as I live. It's not because we don't get along though. I love them. But I can't tell them. I don't know why but I just can't. Maybe it's because of me, I'm too shy and embarrassed to say it. My mom tells my brothers and me that she loves us, but somehow I can't do that. Or maybe it's part of my culture, people (younger generation) of my culture who cannot find the courage to speak face to face with their parents. Maybe it's not that. I don't know, I think it's just based on who I am, if I can someday, I hope to find the courage to say, I love you, to my parents, and to my whole family as well. I know that they can understand the love that is shared in our family.

■ Betty Chang

Sometimes I want to tell my parents what I'm thinking or feeling because I believe they need to know. It seems my parents and I can only talk about certain things. At times when I feel confused and in the need to talk, I usually don't talk to my parents because it might be embarrassing. I don't really feel comfortable talking to my parents because we are not close and I usually don't share my feelings or thoughts with them. Sometimes I think that they don't understand me because it seems like they are never fair to me. My parents tell me things about our culture, but we usually end up arguing. I know that they want me to grow up healthy and well-mannered and I appreciate that. But it's hard to grow up as they wish because we live in America now, and the kids act differently than the kids in Laos and Thailand. Most of the time I wish that my family would not fight over little things. I wish we could be a lot closer.

I usually disagree with my parents, but one day when I am older, I think that I will be able to understand the things that they have been telling me. Even though I don't understand them now, I am very grateful that my parents are here for me, and I will always love them, even though I don't say it very often.

135

■ Va Vang

Sometime I would like to tell my grandmother...sometimes I would like to tell my grandmother...sometimes I would like to tell me grandmother how sweet, how kind, how loveable, and how nice she is. I would like to tell her because she's the only one who cares about me. My parents said that I was a burden to them when they held me.

Life without my grandmother is kind of tough even though I've never seen her, and I don't know what she looks like. Everyday I always think that she is by my side. Every night when I go to sleep, I always think of her. I wish she was still alive today so she could see what I've done in my life. If she was alive I would like to tell her that I love her. I don't know how, or where she died. In life you have to let old memories pass. But, I will not forget my grandmother or my grandfather, both of whom I have never seen.

■ Yee Chang

Sometimes I want to tell my parents that they are the greatest. They have gone through so much; so much that I cannot even begin to understand. I can understand what they say when they tell my how hard life has been for them...and how fortunate we are to be alive, to be living and going to school in America. But, even as I listen to them, I know I can never understand the harsh reality that they endured and survived. I cannot understand the pain and suffering they went through just to put food in our stomach. I cannot understand the year-round toil of slash and burn agriculture. I cannot understand the danger that threatened their lives, forcing them to move from mountain to mountain, hoping to find a safe place for a year, for a month, or maybe for just a day. I cannot understand how they carried us, literally, to freedom. They risked their lives so we could make something of ourselves in this new country. Tears come to my eyes when I realize how much they have suffered.

■ Bruce Xiang

Sometimes I want to tell my parents what we will have to do to get a better life in America. Our life in America is hard. My parents tell me that I should study hard and go to college for four years. They say that after I graduate from college my life will change a lot from what it is now. I won't need Welfare anymore, like I do today.

My parents often tell me to go to school, not to steal, and try to be a good person. I listen to my parents and hear what they have to say. Now that I'm a senior and will graduate in the spring, I think I want to continue my education because I know that it is the key to help me, my family, and the Hmong community.

Hopes for the Future

" My hope for the future is . . . "

■ Shu Yang

Someday I would like to visit Laos and Thailand to find the place in which I was born, and the culture from which I came. Visiting Laos and Thailand would help me to understand who I am, and what values I have.

I would go into the villages to find my relatives who couldn't come to the U.S., as I did. I would learn about everyday people, and how everything is done. I would learn about the lives of my parents, and be inspired to grow, to know where I'm from. There would be many differences in Thailand and Laos, but, for some people, the old ways are much better.

■ Paul Yang

Late at night I sometimes think about my future. I think about what I'll be doing for the next 10 years. I have many thoughts about what I should be doing in high school, in college, after college, and in pursuit of a career. Imagining myself in a certain career or position makes me head in that direction. I have two main goals, but I know that I must choose only one.

I want to be either a physicist-astronomer, or a comic-book artist. I feel that I have strong interests in both areas.

When I think about school, I think about how well I'm doing, what I've learned so far, and how I can use that knowledge to help me find my way in this country. I rarely think about my past, but when I do, I put a lot of energy into it. I think about how far I've made it through life, and how far I have to go. I study my past, and use it to guide me along the pathway of life.

■ Va Vang

The hope for the Hmong in the future is that they would live in their own country. They would feel a lot happier than living in America. I hope most of the generation will go to college. What I know about the future now is that a lot of our generation are joining gangs. To stop this habit, we must ask what they need. If these kids stop this we would have a better chance keeping our lives safer. In the future, if we care for, or love each other and join in together we would have better chance of living in our own country.

My life is hard now because of pressure about going to school. I hope that I would get a good education. I hope to go to college, then

137

get my master's degree. As I think about the future, I realize these dreams might never come true. I also hope, one day, to play football for part of my career. I always dream to have what is true and what is not. Well, life is nothing as I think it is, but if you put a lot of thought into it you would know what life is. I would like all gang members to take a look at themselves to see who they are, and to stop killing each other. I hope they know that they're also Hmong. If this ever happens in the future, the Hmong people would live in a better place and be more successful than have been in the past. I hope one day all the Hmong people would join hands together and live peacefully in their own country. This is the dream I hope for the future.

■ Paul Yang

In the future I would like to draw comics for Image Comics because I love comic books and comic book art. I also like the characters. I feel that Image Comics is the doorway to my future.

My main ambition is to work alongside Jim Lee, Todd McFarlane, Marc Silvestri, and the rest of the Image crew. These people have inspired me to draw and create my own characters. Many Hmong kids, like my friend Koua Lee, are really into comic books. He and I love to talk about comic books. He has similar goals as me. Maybe in the next five years I will be able to work alongside him, as well.

I know that drawing characters is a hard job, but also very satisfying.

■ Shu Yang

In the future, I think, the Hmong culture will eventually vanish and the language could possibly become a dead language. If we don't so something about it, the future might not have a lot of Hmong things in it . Teenagers today don't seem interested in preserving their culture, and only the elders emphasize it. When the elders are gone, the culture will go with them.

I might try to preserve our culture, but might not have the ingredients for the recipe to keep it alive. Many people are converting to Christianity and the Hmong culture contradicts the Christian way of life. This is another factor contributing to the loss of our culture.

We're also losing our culture because Hmong teenagers don't value who they are, and are not proud to be Hmong. ▼

138

Epilogue

For the old

In Hmong folk tales, there is a story of a man who crawled out of the earth with a flower. The seeds of the flower brought to the world the corn, the rice, the people, the animals, and the sun and the moon. But, where is that flower to be found in America? My mother tells me that we (the children) were the reasons they had to risk their lives to cross the river to Thailand. They often remind us children how their backs ached from the heavy toils of life on the mountains of Laos. They say they are old and cannot accomplish much with their bare hands in this new and strange land. Most of the parents of first generation Hmongs in the U.S. have never had any formal education. Their tongues are tied by the letters R and S that they think make up the English language. The lines on their faces run deep with age, bearing the marks of struggle and survival. Their feet are now bound by American shoes that don't fit, and they find themselves immobile and confused in this urban, technological, and systematic society.

They did not choose to come to America. It was their only choice for a better life, or just plain life itself.

The Hmong no longer have to wait for the seasons of slash-and-burn agriculture and then fear their harvest lost to wars which permeated and destroyed their livelihood. The Hmong are now free from being hunted down and exterminated by the communists who targeted them in revenge for helping the Americans during the Vietnam War.

In the U.S., life has been better for the Hmong. For the first time in history, all of their children now have the one chance they never had or imagined possible; to go to school, "to learn so that the Hmong people can catch up with the other human races," General Vang Pao said at the 1992-93 Hmong New Year Celebration in St. Paul.

In the United States, the Hmong are at last free from political persecution, free from immediate physical threat of death. But under their skin and in their conscience, they remain imprisoned by the cultural barriers and different values of this country. Sometimes, they lose a sense of themselves as worthy and competent members of the community because they lack the skills to succeed. Their roles as respected elders in the community have been dramatically altered. They have become dependent on their children and outside sources for support.

139

For the young

The Hmong children face many barriers growing up in a new land. Throughout our history, and everywhere we went, we have had to deal with questions about our identity. What does it mean to be a Hmong growing up in the U.S.? We must again define who we are, this time among overwhelming social, economic and political forces which we have little control over.

Today, to be a Hmong in the eyes of the Hmong community of parents and elders is to be fluent in Hmong, have respect for elders, participate in family celebrations and help each other when we need help. To be Hmong is having the will to succeed in a country of opportunities while maintaining one's identity. When young people get so involved and take up a false caricature of the American culture, they widen the gap between them and their elders. Today, people look at me and think I am "Americanized." Almost all of my time in school is spent speaking, writing and thinking in English. I like to watch television and listen to American music. But there are times when I know I have to get back to being Hmong. Education is important in helping me get back to my roots. I learn about myself, the world and my place in it as a person. Education allows me to become a Hmong American. ▼

❝ What I learned … ❞

■ Moo Vu

I learned a lot of stuff that I didn't even know such as the Hmong culture, folk tales, the religion, the Hmong house, and music and much more. The project I did a subject on hunting and fishing. I had to ask an older person questions about like what kind of guns did they use and ho many animals they shot--stuff like that. And then my next subject was Boy scouts. I just asked them what they did in Boy scouts and stuff. I picked those topics because for hunting and fishing what if you go back to Laos and you don't know how to hunt. And for Boy Scouts I think every boy should join Boy Scout because it teaches you a lot of stuff such as cooking, lashing, first-aid, swimming and stuff. So I think that HYCAP is very fun and I learned a lot.

■ Kao Vang

During HYCAP I learned a lot. I learned how to do interviews, I developed better writing skills, and I got to know more about the Hmong culture .

On my interviews I did shamanism and I learned a lot on what a shaman does during the ritual. I learned h ow the shaman talks to the spirits in the spirit world and cures the patient. I'm very glad theat I was a part in writing this book.

■ Va Vang

I think I learned how to write and interview people. I think its fun coming to HYCAP because you meet a lot of people, and its fun to talk to them.

■ Tong Thao

In writing this book with all the HYCAP members, I gained a lot of experiences that could, in a way, help me prepare for whatever that has to do with publishing, researching, interviewing, and many other ink-shedding activities.

Also, from this experience with the rest of the HYCAP process, if I ever want to write a book, I would have this experience to prepare for it.

Interviewing, researching, and writing accounts of experiences about my people, as well as my origin, was fascinating!

■ Mai See Xiong

When I first heard about this project I was interested in it very much. I learned from this project how to interview people, how to write stories about the Hmong culture, and get to know more about my culture. I learned about how the Hmong people build their own houses.

■ Chua Chang

HYCAP was fun. I learned a lot of new things and I learned a lot of things from the interviews that I did on the Hmong houses. The interview was hard to do like we had to think up questions and then in-terviews the person, then translate it. It took a lot of my free time away and I was kind of angry, but I knew that I had to finish it before I could have any free time and I was glad when it was finally over, and we handed it in. I am glad that I joined this group and learned new things.

■ Pang Xiong

I joined the Hmong Youth Cultural Awareness Project in the Fall of 1993. I have learned a lot from the HYCAP group, and had a lot of fun, too. I think its very nice that this project is being held because I and the other students could meet new people and make new friends through the project.

■ Mai Nhia Xiong

When I first heard about this project I really got interested in it. Since I don't really know much about the Hmong culture, I decided to join this class. Ever since I've been in this project, I've learned a lot of things about our culture from interviews I did and from people I met and things I saw. This project wasn't as fun as I expected, and I don't know how I managed to make it through. It was like being at school, in a class learning your own culture, and even getting homework. But I guess it was sure a lot of fun being here. And I guess I'll probably miss this class when its over.

■ Betty Chang

I learned a lot from being in HY-CAP. I learned about my family's struggle to get here and the pain and suffering they went through. I not only learned about my family, but others too. I learned of their family's struggle. I learned their thoughts and dreams and what it feels like to be Hmong in America. We're Hmong and on the same side. If I never joined this group I would not know these things; I'm pretty grateful I did. ▼